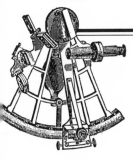
sextant

Said one retired Sea Captain,
"ANY MAN WHO WOULD GO TO SEA FOR PLEASURE WOULD GO TO HELL FOR A PASTIME."

There is every indication that Brewster sea men did indeed take great pleasure in going to sea . . . pleasure in the constant challenges . . . pleasure in overcoming apparently insurmountable problems . . . pleasure in the dangers of unfamiliar, uncharted seas . . . and keenest of all pleasures, being in command, in complete control. Brewster Sea Captains were pleasured to a point suspiciously close to addiction. For no matter how horrendous the previous voyage, they eagerly returned for the next, and welcomed whatever adventures it held in store for them.

Even in a Cape Cod environment which strongly fostered individuality, the uncommon talents of Brewster sea men were held to be especially valuable by shipping companies, and much sought after. They were incomparable at what they did; canny traders, with an astonishing ability to cope with all circumstances at sea or in business. They were highly motivated, profit driven, record driven, glory driven. They were men of such talents that even today, after the passing of nearly two centuries, their stories still fire our imagination with wonder.

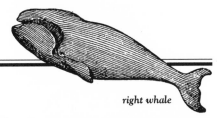
right whale

1

Logged

CAPE COD
MASTERS *of the* SEAS

EXTRAORDINARY TALES OF
BREWSTER'S SHIPMASTERS
& PACKET CAPTAINS

BY JOAN PAINE

Book Design by Joan Paine

WRACKLINE WRITERS ©2000

Aboard

WHO BUT A BREWSTER SHIPMASTER would think of loading aboard a cargo of ice and sailing with it down to the tropics, to a surprised and profitable market? Later on this same Captain would bring in the first shipload of wild animals for P.T. Barnum's Circus. Just the sort of individual the great P.T. would appreciate.

Brewster's J. Henry Sears, already a Shipmaster at 24, once commanded a ship transporting French troops and munitions to the Crimean War. Shortly thereafter he was freighting a record-breaking load of 6,900 bales of cotton from New Orleans to Liverpool. Then he was off with a load of colonists Australia bound. All in a day's work for men like Sears.

Another Shipmaster long gone, but still an icon among Brewster people, ran embargoed rum into Ireland in the most politically correct way, paying off appropriate officials with a bit of money and a bit more rum. Had you asked him about the honorability of such activities, he would have said he operated more by the laws of God than those of men. (And the law of dollar exchange was most important of all.)

Many a Brewster Shipmaster had a run-in with pirates. Well into the 1800s our coastal waters were infested by pirates and privateers (who were little more than upper-class pirates with government Letters of Marque authorizing them to capture and rob any vessel on the high seas with which their country had political differences. Of course, in return for such valuable papers, the government got its share of the booty.) No wonder, then, that a community with such a vibrant tradition of imagination, ingenuity and courage takes great pride in being known as the Sea Captains Town.

Back in 1806 the local Pastor, John Simpkins, observed that "more than three-quarters of the inhabitants, as they come forward upon the stage (of life) are employed at sea. The greatest part of them are merchantmen. There are more Masters and Mates of vessels who sail on foreign voyages, belonging to this place, than any other

4

town in the country." In his book *Brewster Shipmasters*, J. Henry Sears says, "From a population numbering about one thousand people we have the names of one hundred and fifteen Shipmasters living since the year 1840 – and during the year 1850 there were over fifty living there at one time."

It just could be that this rate of success in Shipmastering was due in part to Brewster's pioneering school system. Parson Simpkins went on to say that "the residents have for some years maintained a man's school throughout the year . . . they regularly subscribe $3,000 toward the academy's support." The "man's school" would have given Brewster boys intensive courses in astronomy, navigation, mathematics, chart making and reading, and probably a good grounding in trading and money management. For these lads, some turned Captains at 20 or so, were often totally responsible for buying and selling cargoes for their shipping companies. They themselves often owned shares in their voyages, an added incentive to make each trip as richly rewarding as possible.

There is no mention that the academy gave courses in bonesetting, tooth pulling, or suturing. With or without training, the ship's Master was indeed also the ship's Doctor, and the ship's Minister of the Faith who, failing in his medical practice, could give the late patient a decent Christian burial at sea. The ship's Master also kept the records of trade, recording the contents of cargoes, how they sold, what the market was looking for and whether to return with more of the same. It was the Master who noted errors in the imperfect and limited sailing charts of the times. Later such information would be incorporated into Nathaniel Bowditch's *Navigation*, the bible of every Captain, to tell him where he was and what to look out for. As Bowditch described his book, it was "The New American Practical Navigator, Being an Epitomy of Navigation."

Brewster's Sea Captains and Shipmasters were a breed apart. The positions they held required them to assume awesome responsibilities for the safety of their men, their ships and their cargoes.

Bestowed upon them was absolute authority when running the ship. The title of Shipmaster was hard won and of the greatest honor.

A host of men from Cape towns were sailing up and down the Atlantic coast, and back and forth across the oceans between 1785 and the late 1800s . . . the same years that saw Brewster Shipmasters rounding the Horn for Canton and other mysterious and exotic ports. But only a very few of these men left any accounts of themselves to show us what manner of life they lived in the tremendously competitive and generally disordered seaport markets of other continents. Even the most diligent search for facts may render only the meager words of church or mortuary records.

But even with such a scarcity of information, reading the personal accounts of those who did leave records brings their stories to life. And provides even the least-known among them proud, strong identities.

IT WAS CUSTOMARY when the Shipmaster was about to sail, for him to receive orders in writing, spelling out the company or owner's expectations of him. Orders could be in great detail or as terse and to the point as those received by one Captain: "My *object is to make money with as little risk and as much dispatch as possible.*"

"Nestling since yesterday at her cozy quarters in South Boston, the barque *W.H. Besse*, from Manila, the first that has reached us with vivid realization of the volcanic eruptions in Asia, gives little indication of the extraordinary perils through which she has passed." So wrote a Boston newspaper man in 1884, reporting that demonic voyage, with information gleaned from the log book of

SHIPMASTER BENJAMIN C. BAKER 1841 – unknown

"After forty days spent in the capital of the largest island, Manila, where Capt. Baker's vessel suffered the loss of several seamen by the epidemic of cholera, the *W.H. Besse* set sail for Boston on the 27th of May. The Macassar Straits were soon reached with light and variable winds. At 5 p.m. on June 24, she struck a coral reef which had not yet been found on any chart. The pumps were set to work, but they were unable to start off the reef until 11 p.m. The vessel began to fill and it was found necessary to heave over a portion of the cargo (sugar). After letting go of the port anchor and getting the lifeboats ready, the whole power of those on board was required to keep out the water during the night. At midnight the men were exhausted and the pumping was stopped. Happily, on the 26th, a Dutch steamer came up and succeeded in starting the bark off toward Batavia (for repairs)." The steamer supplied 40 Chinese laborers, (possibly passengers on the steamer) to man the *Besse's* pumps 'round the clock until she reached Batavia on the 27th of June.

In Batavia the barque was repaired and new supplies put aboard, which took about 2 months. This all sounds like a happy ending to a near disaster for Capt. Baker. In fact, his strange odyssey was just beginning. The records of his log continue, as reported by the journalist.

"Having sailed toward the Straits of Sundra, on the 26th of August light airs and calms were met. Throughout the afternoon and night heavy reports were heard like the discharge of heavy artillery. It became very dark and cloudy through the night with continued and countless flashes of lightning. Monday, August 27, opened with strong breezes and thick, cloudy weather. Since day-break a dark, heavy bank had been noticed, which continued to rise, the sun was obscured and the whole heavens black. All hands were called on deck, every bit of canvas furled, the port anchor let go, and Capt. Baker awaited a catastrophe. Scarcely had the sails and anchor been disposed of when a squall struck the side of the barque with terrific force. With the squall came heavy showers of sand and ashes. The atmosphere was darker than the darkest night. The barometer continued to rise and fall an inch at a time. The wind blew a hurricane and the water was lashed into a tumultuous motion. A heavy rumbling, with reports like steadily increasing thunder, continued and the awful blackness overhead was made still more appalling by the lurid and fitful lightning that flashed in jagged yet concentric streaks. Although still daylight, there was not enough light to see one's hand. A stinking smell of sulphur filled the whole atmosphere making it difficult to do the amount of breathing necessary to sustain consciousness. The tide was set-ting strongly to the west, and the barque rushed along under bare poles at a rate of 14 knots an hour. The sounds and scenes through all the hours of day and night were of the most awful description. The shrieking wind, the spuming and churning waves, the murky and impenetrable veil overhead and on every side, that threat-ened to engulf the fated vessel, combined to daze and appall every soul on board. There was spread the common feeling of some ca-tastrophe, and the sense of disturbance in nature beyond any ex-perience of a mariner. Several were sure that the day of final judg-ment had come.

"At 3 p.m. the sky began to grow a little lighter although ashes and other volcanic matter continued to fall. The barometer rose and fell rapidly and then became stationary. The whole ship, rig-ging and masts, were coated with sand and ashes the depth of sev-eral inches."

Capt. Baker, the *W.H. Besse* and her crew had just lived through the stupendous eruption of Indonesia's Krakatau volcano in 1883.

The volcanic activity continued through August 26, 27 and 28, with the reported loss of 36,000 lives. Capt. Baker saw vast quantities of trees and dead fish floating by with the tide, the water having a whitish appearance caused by the surface of light ash.

"It was soon discovered that mighty changes had been wrought in the outlines of sea and shore, whole islands had sunk, the entire northwest part of Krakatau Island had disappeared, and the beautiful forest-clothed islands of Lang and Verlaten had been completely denuded.

"August 28 came in calm, thick murky weather. Immense masses of coconuts, trees, fish were encountered, the debris extending over more than 500 miles. In the afternoon no lighthouse or sign of life could be discerned.

"All light sails were furled, and the barque stood out under easy sail through the night. On August 30, the water was covered with large trees and driftwood, it being almost impossible to steer clear of them. A lookout was kept in the forecastle through the day and masses of dead bodies were passed.

"On August 31 four seamen were off duty on account of Java fever; the remainder of the crew were kept engaged in clearing ashes off the rigging. On September 7, a severe squall struck the ship and the deck was flooded fore and aft. Good sailing then prevailed until November 26; a heavy swell from the northwest was felt and flashes of lightning were seen in the north. At 2 a.m. the next morning the sky was lit from southwest to southeast and, the storm increasing rapidly, all hands were called on deck, all sails furled and hatches battened down. A strong gale came on which increased to a hurricane, and a topsail was lost.

"For several days the gale continued and it was necessary to extend lifelines fore and aft in order to protect the crew who were almost prostrated by their exertions at the pumps. Seventy-five tons of sugar were thrown overboard in order to protect the ship."

Of a crew of 22 aboard Capt. Baker's ship, when she sailed from Manilla some five months earlier, only five men were available to work the barque *W.H. Besse* when tugs towed her up Boston Harbor. Two were lying sick when she reached the wharf in South Boston, and late in the afternoon one man, not expected to live through the night, was sent to the hospital.

In the space of one voyage Shipmaster Benjamin Baker and the *W.H. Besse* had lived through an odyssey which seems more like a Hollywood adventure than the terrible reality it was. They had survived **(1.)** a cholera epidemic **(2.)** striking fast on a coral reef **(3.)** a near sinking as the result **(4.)** the explosion of Krakatau, one of the world's greatest volcanic disasters **(5.)** a hurricane **(6.)** a shortage of hands to manage the ship, due to sickness aboard. But in the best tradition of Brewster Shipmasters, Capt. Baker brought his ship back home.

T**HEY KNEW, BUT DID THEY FULLY KNOW,** Captain Baker and the crew of the *W.H. Besse* (a jinxed ship if ever there was one), how near they had been to the end of their days in that shrieking, roaring, living hell on earth they were to witness up close? That is, as close as one could get and still have the slightest chance of survival . . . that being several miles distant. What the Captain was logging in his book was the horrifying, literally world-shaking explosion of the 2,640-foot high Krakatau volcano, in 1883.

Until that August 26th, Krakatau had been a lush green forested volcanic island located in the Sundra Strait between Sumatra and Java. Then, with an ominous roar, Krakatau sent a flood of pyroclastic flows of hot rocks and rubble pouring down its slopes, to bury some 2,000 islanders.

But that was, comparatively, just a murmured threat from Krakatau. The following day, August 27, the whole island thundered into a mega blast of erupting flames, gasses, and black clouds of lightning-shot volcanic ash and dust . . . a cosmic roar heard 2,500 miles away . . . an explosion to dwarf that of an atomic bomb.

Volcanic dusts hoisted high into Earth's atmosphere would be blown around the globe to affect world weather patterns for several years to come.

The force of such an explosion can result in an abrupt drop in atmospheric pressure. Coupled with the shaking and displacement of the ocean floor it will spawn a tremendous tsunami tidal wave, sucking back the waters even to bare-bottoming the sea floor in places, piling the seas into a monstrous mountain of water. Forming a towering bulge in the ocean, hundreds of miles long and 60, 80, 100 feet and more high, Krakatau's tsunami spanned the great Pacific, swept across low lying islands and drowned continental coastal areas for miles inland, and affected sea levels as far away as the British Isles.

Cold statistics say 36,000 people died. They do not mention how they died . . . buried alive in debris . . . asphyxiated with sulphurous gasses, or by life's breath being barometrically sucked out of their lungs . . . or those blown away by the blast . . . or drowned in the maelstrom of ocean waters rushing in to fill the 1,000-foot deep crater blasted into the sea bed when mighty Krakatau blew and sank. Nor do stastics list the thousands more, unknown and uncounted, drowned on tsunami submerged coastal areas hundreds of miles away, and swept into the ocean from inundated islands. Or those dead of disease or starvation, the aftermath of the devastation.

Then there was a long silence. The Krakatau catastrophe was mostly forgotten .. until 1927 when a volcanic mound gradually emerged from where it had sunk 74 years earlier . . . rising above the waters like the monster of the deep it was, being pressured upwards by the Pacific ring of Earth's inner fires. A new island formed, briefly to be called Anak Krakatau, which then exploded in 1929, sinking back into the cradle created by Krakatau's 1883 eruption. As recently as 1995 this scene was again repeated.

Almost certainly the world will see Krakatau emerge yet again. And those Captains who keep the logs will witness its presence with understandable trepidation.

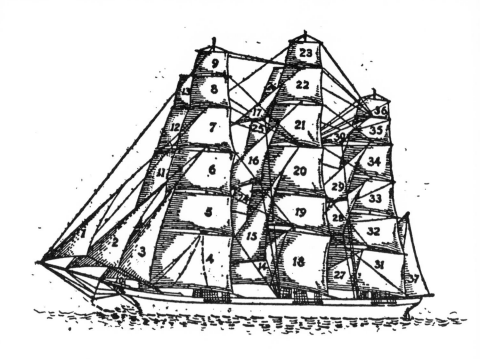

FULL-RIGGED SHIP UNDER ALL PLAIN SAIL

1. Flying Jib **2.** Jib **3.** Fore-topmast Staysail **4.** Foresail
5. Lower Fore-topsail **6.** Upper Fore-topsail **7.** Fore-topgallant
Sail **8.** Foreroyal **9.** Fore-skysail **10.** Lower Studding Sail
11. Fore-topmast Studding Sail **12.** Fore-topgallant Studding
Sail **13.** Foreroyal Studding Sail **14.** Main Staysail **15.** Main-
topmast Staysail **16.** Main-topgallant Staysail **17.** Main-royal
Staysail **18.** Mainsail **19.** Lower Main Topsail **20.** Upper Main
Topsail **21.** Main-topgallant Sail **22.** Main Royal **23.** Main
Skysail **24.** Main-topmast Studding Sail **25.** Main-topgallant
Studding Sail **26.** Main-royal Studding Sail **27.** Mizzen Staysail
28. Mizzen-topmast Staysail **29.** Mizzen-topgallant Staysail
30. Mizzen-royal Staysail **31.** Mizzen Sail **32.** Lower Mizzen
Topsail **33.** Upper Mizzen Topsail **34.** Mizzen-topgallant Sail
35. Mizzen Royal **36.** Mizzen Skysail **37.** Spanker

He was a veritable Neptune of a man, a man with great capacity to succeed, to survive . . . and to surprise!

SHIPMASTER J. HENRY SEARS 1829 – 1912

Consider the seeming incongruity of a 19th century Sea Captain as avid golfer. Captain Sears had a private golf course, with a club house that looked out to sea from a high point on his 32 acres of sandy property on Lower Road in Brewster. The town called it Lobster Lane back then. And there was another unexpected persona . . . Sears had a private bowling alley in a barn sort of building behind his fine Main Street home. Golfer, bowler, country squire . . . not exactly how you picture a driver of ships and men . . . one who, in his day, probably contributed more to the prosperity of the Town of Brewster than did any other of her renowed Shipmasters. J. Henry Sears was an amazing multi-faceted figure.

A defining moment for the young Captain (already a 12-year veteran of the sea at age 24) finds him London bound on the ship *Titan*, heavily laden with a cargo of Peruvian guano (the prime source of high nitrogen fertilizer back in those days). *Titan* is caught in a raging storm. She's a young ship, only 3 years old, and should be able to cope. But she has been over-cargoed and over-driven all her few years, and now comes the reckoning. Her seams are sprung and she is leaking irreversably. The nearest land is Brazil, 1,100 miles away. Young Captain Sears must now prove whether he is worthy of the title "Shipmaster".

It is an agonizing decision he must make. Should he and his crew risk riding it out aboard *Titan* with the hope that by some miracle *Titan* can make port and save her valuable cargo? This, after all, is Sears' primary responsibility to his employers. Or should his responsibility for the lives of his crew take precedence, with an order to abandon ship before she goes down taking them all with her? Leaving the ship has its own great risks. In such wind-driven seas it can be almost impossible to launch the life boats, and often fatal to try boarding them as they are tossed in mountainous waves.

Finally all hands safely abandon ship and set sail in their open life boats, hoping to reach Rio de Janeiro. A week of struggling finds them still fighting for their lives. Then, by some fluke of luck, a Spanish vessel sights the desperate flotilla, picks up the lot and sets them back on terra firma, Brazil.

In his seagoing life Sears probably saw and knew more of England, and France and South America, and other far-away ports, than he did of his Cape Cod home. For at 12 he was off to sea as a cabin boy, where he not only served his Captain well but thoroughly absorbed the skills to master ships and lead men. In fact, so reliable and quick to learn was Sears that he earned his first command when he was only 22. Is was the fine ship *Faneuil Hall* in the European trade. Only two years later he was racing the fabled clipper *Wild Ranger* to San Francisco. That trip would take him twice around Cape Horn, a notoriously stormy and dangerous passage that only the most stalwart, skilled, and brave-hearted Masters would attempt.

J. Henry Sears would meet all these challenges and go on to sail through eight more adventurous years before he retired in 1861, at age 32 to embark on a new land based career as head of the J.H. Sears Shipping Company, Port of Boston. Over the years his register of vessels would include 37 fullrigged ships carrying all manner of cargo to ports around the world. Sears would be the number one employer of Brewster men, with a roster of some 35 to 40 Shipmasters chosen from the best of the best Brewster Masters.

J. Henry Sears made Brewster his final home port when he retired in 1898, to enjoy his golf course and bowling alley. And here, in 1906, he wrote his book *Brewster Shipmasters*. Today a collectors' item, it is a treasury of vital information in the all too sparce record of Brewster's glory years at sea.

Captain Sears was a major sponsor and activist in the movement to memorialize the place where the Pilgrims first landed in Provincetown on Cape Cod. He lived to see the Provincetown Monument completed and dedicated in 1910.

BREWSTER'S FIRST GOLF CLUBHOUSE ?

J. Henry Sears' clubhouse was also headquarters for the Pilgrim Club of Brewster when it and the Cape Cod Memorial Association merged their efforts to sponsor the building of the Provincetown Monument. Sears stands first man at the right in this picture.

On a clear day you can see the towering granite monument all the way across Cape Cod Bay from Brewster's Breakwater Beach. And at night it becomes a bright shaft of light in the dark sky. Perhaps when you see it you will be reminded not only of the rugged Pilgrims who first settled this land, but of the extraordinary man whose life set a standard of accomplishment that was remarkable even for that distinguished breed of sea men known as Brewster Shipmasters.

YANKEE TRADING ability knew no limits. Coastal skippers wrote of swapping barrel staves for mahogany in the West Indies trade.

Pitting his smart little clipper *Shooting Star* against the challenge of acknowledged racing master Josiah Richardson's great 240 foot clipper ship *Staffordshire*,

SHIPMASTER JUDAH BAKER 1807 – 1853

clears Boston Harbor the same day as Richardson. Their destination, San Francisco. Though smaller than *Staffordshire*, *Star* has the advantage of sharper lines and is one of the fastest in her class. Challenges like this one are not new to Baker. Already he has distinguished himself in the trade as a worthy rival of any Shipmaster.

After three months at sea, after the trials of beating around the Horn, the two vessels finish only four days apart. *Staffordshire* comes foaming into San Francisco Bay in 101 days, *Shooting Star* in 105. It is actually a triumph for the reputations of both their Masters, for it will put their services in even greater demand among shippers and shipping companies.

This was not the only fine run Capt. Baker had made on *Shooting Star*. He had gone 'round the world with her on her maiden voyage in 1851. In the course if this trip he had lost his main topgallant mast, and had put into Rio for repairs. But even with this delay, he came roaring home to Boston from Macao in just 86 days.

In the summer of 1853 Capt. Baker is commissioned to take another spanking new clipper, *Flying Dragon*, on her maiden voyage from Boston to San Francisco. The trip goes well, the Captain and his new charge getting to know each others' demands . . . until they reach Cape Horn. There, week after week Capt. Baker struggles to drive *Flying Dragon* westward against the tumultuous seas, cold and miserable weather, and overpowering currents. *Flying Dragon's* bowsprit and fore yard are sprung and her jib boom carried away. Even as he finally rounds Cape Horn and safely passes over the Equator, Capt. Baker has lost his own race. The strain has sapped his spirit and his health; he dies before reaching San Francisco.

S PEAKING OF THE TERRIBLE TRIALS of rounding Cape Horn, Kittredge, in his book *Shipmasters of Cape Cod*, says that as the demand for clipper ships grew, with their capacity to make fast trips, (even then speed was money) racing around Cape Horn became a sort of national sport, and few were the Shipmasters who did not test their mettle over this great course.

Back then, rounding the Horn was the only way to get to Pacific ports, and would be until 1914 when the Panama Canal was finally opened for business. The first ship to pass through the canal, one hot August day, took only 8 hours to travel from the Atlantic side to the Pacific. Thus an unparalleled era of sea history came to an end . . . amazing that men could drive themselves and their sailing ships on such a sea course . . . appalling in the toll it took.

Cape Cod Shipmasters were rounding the Horn heading for Canton as early as 1780. In so doing they created one of the most colorful and important chapters in our country's history. Unfortunately, few left any records of themselves or their trips.

SHIPMASTER ELISHA BANGS 1805 – 1886

was one of these almost anonymous Brewster Masters. He had to be a sea man of considerable ability, for he commanded the ships *Rajah, Denmark, Crimea,* and *Faneuil Hall* for the J.H. Sears Shipping Company. Sears would have commissioned only the ablest. For if a ship burned, or was wrecked, or if her Master brought her back without a full purse of profits, the loss could be disastrous for the shipping line. Insurance would pay only a miniscule part of the value lost.

Faneuil Hall was one of the early clippers, built in Medford, Massachusetts. She was slim and sharp of line and a very fast sailer in the hands of a driver like Bangs. What sort of voyages did Bangs make on her? His records may be lost to us, but the configuration of his ship speaks loud and clear of adventure and danger. *Faneuil Hall* was built with 9 gun ports on each side, designed to discourage any Chinese or Malay pirates Bangs might encounter. A fine example of Yankee thrift and ingenuity, *Faneuil Hall's* gun ports were realistic fakes!

Elisha Bangs beat the law of sea averages which tell us that about one third of those who went down to the sea in ships would be lost on it. Shipmaster Elisha Bangs died ashore at the age of 81. His name lives on, for the Town of Brewster has a street named Capt. Bangs Road. And a brass plate marks the pew where he sat when attending services at the Brewster's First Parish Church.

BARKS, BARQUES
& BARKENTINES

Many small sailing vessels were included under these classifications. Basically, a bark had three masts. The foremast and mainmast were square rigged. The mizzenmast carried no yards; there was a hoist-and-lower fore-and-aft sail, and a gaff topsail.

A few ambitiously designed four and five-masted barks were built. Usually they were iron hulled because a wooden vessel could break in two under the strain of the additional length required to accommodate one or two added masts and their rigging which, in themselves, added a backbreaking weight.

It was very obvious to the home office that this 22-year-old First Mate had all the energy and expertise needed to step directly into the boots of his commander. And that is how

SHIPMASTER WILLIAM BURGESS 1829 – c.1854

came to be in charge of the slow, old East Indiaman named *Herbert*, heading out of Boston one breezy September day in 1851, Pacific bound. This time the old ship is going to see some changes made. Burgess is an impatient "driver". In a week he reports back that a "brisk SSE breeze" has carried away his flying jib boom and split the sail-ends. What's more, he finds the three ship's compasses all point in different directions. He corrects the binnacle compass to the proper variations for his position. Then sends old *Herbert* plowing ahead to the best of her ability, course set for Calcutta. She makes it in just 119 days. Impatiently he loads with the usual East India staples, faces *Herbert* out of the harbor and goads her back to Boston in 115 days . . . four days better than the outward trip.

You sense his impatience to get on with something more challenging when he writes in his log, "So ends the voyage of the ship *Herbert*, W.H. Burgess Master – from Boston to Calcutta and back again performing the same in 10 months to the day . . ."

Get on with it he does. He is soon in command of the new clipper *Whirlwind* on her maiden voyage to San Francisco and back. Then, signed on line for additional trips with *Whirlwind*, he brings aboard his new wife who will prove to be as canny as her husband in the ways of great ships.

Her first task is to cure him from cursing, which she does, although it is not at all sure that a balky ship can be handled with expletives deleted. However, Burgess brings *Whirlwind* back to New York and there turns her over to another Master, while he and his wife step onto the quarter deck of the clipper *Challenger*, and head for San Francisco. There Burgess receives orders to pick up a cargo of guano at the Chincha Islands off Peru. Not long after, he is taken ill and cannot leave his berth. The only reliable doctor is 22 sailing days away. *Challenger's* Mate is able to "shoot the sun" but cannot work out the ship's positions. So Mrs. Burgess makes the calculations and together they navigate *Challenger* to Valparaiso. But the race is lost. Captain Burgess dies 48 hours before they make port.

Even in the face of this disaster, Mrs. Burgess remains in charge and arranges for herself and her husband's body to be brought back home on another vessel. One wonders how well the Mate made out in setting *Challenger's* course homeward bound without Mrs. Burgess's calculations.

CORSETS WERE DE RIGUEUR, back in the 1800s, for any Brewster lady who <u>was</u> a lady, even when she was on a sea voyage with her Shipmaster husband. This could pose a problem. For corsets were reinforced with steel stays. And the most advanced navigational technology of the day was based on the accuracy of the ship's compass. So the ladies were warned to steer clear of the binnacle lest their corset stays magnetize the compass.

SHROUDS & RATLINES
Shroud ropes are rigged from a vessel's mastheads to deck level, to give lateral support to the masts. Ratlines are small, tarred ropes traversing the shrouds and forming a rope ladder.

DO NOT THINK FOR A MOMENT THAT raucous claims about who is number one are an invention of today's wonder world of advertising. Even in the technological dark ages of the 18th and 19th centuries, the CEOs of the shipping lines fired desire with an imaginative one-upmanship in naming ships.

For instance, there were the birds: *White Swallow, Nightingale, Raven, National Eagle* (a name of double irresistibility), *Carrier Pigeon, Fleetwing, Skylark* . . . a whole flight of fancies that assured you if you really wanted fast delivery you could choose no other vessel.

There were the wild ones: *Wild Ranger, Wild Rover, Wild Hunter, Wild Wave*, suggesting an adventurous derring-do attitude that would get you and your shipment anywhere, and damn the pirates, full speed ahead.

Then there were those blessed with a special mastery of the sea: *Belle of the Sea, Sea Serpent, Empress of the Sea, Gem of the Ocean*. Surely any ship so named could conquer King Neptune himself, and calm the raging waters of the Horn.

And there were those way ahead of their time: *Electra* and *Electric Spark*.

Some names commanded special respect: *Imperial, Rajah, Black Prince, Mogul*, ordained to place your shipping a step higher in the social strata of sea transportation.

Other names like *Morning Star, Antelope, Robin Hood, Southern Cross, Sunshine, Lightfoot, Climax*, speak of great expectations and ambitions that must surely have been disappointed often in the harsh reality of world shipping in the 19th century.

And then there was the ship *Brewster*, surely the first choice among citizens of that Cape Cod town hailed by the same name, providing she was going their way.

Most of all, these names and hundreds of others recorded in ships' registers, reflect the boundless self-assurance, optimism and drive of the new entrepreneurial America. Reading a bit of the history of Brewster Masters and their ships provides a unique perspective on how Americans in general were approaching their recently declared independence . . . their supreme confidence in pushing new opportunities to the limit while discovering, via a pretty much uncharted route, who they really were and where they were planning to go.

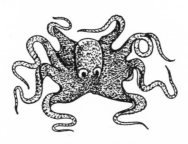

COMMON OCTOPUS
A member of the order of eight-armed dubranchiate cephalopods. Ancient mariners told fearful tales of ships being entangled by giant octopus and dragged down into the deep.

One of the curious inconsistencies of maritime vocabulary was the custom of calling any freighting vessel a merchantman, when every sailor knew every ship was a she.

". . . the first time I went down the long wharf and stood gazing at a new vessell, wondering, and admiring her monsterous size, her great cables and anchors etc – a gentleman stept from her deck and thus accosted me. My lad do you want a voyage – where are you bound Sir – to Siranam – I am told Sir, that all flesh die that go there – well my boy, to prove that you have not been told the truth, I have been there 13 voyages and you see I'm alive yet – well Sir, I should like to go, what wages will you allow me – do you know how to cook – not much Sir, but I can soon learn – well my boy, if you think so I presume you will. I will take you, and give you the customary wages of a boy $3.40 pr. month, but you must go immediately on board and git dinner for the men – and thus I commenced my duty as cook and cabin boy." So wrote

SHIPMASTER ELIJAH COBB 1768 – 1848

His father had died at sea leaving an impoverished widow and six children. Elijah, the youngest, was only 6 when his mother, desperate to feed her children, sent him to live with another family, there to work for his keep. Then, when he was 13, he walked to Orleans and sailed to Boston on the schooner *Creture*. Local lore says he paid his fare with a couple of bushels of dried corn. He would have had to be a stout lad indeed, for a bushel of properly dried corn weighs about 56 pounds; it would be quite a challenge to tote two bushels to Orleans.

There can be not the slightest doubt that Cobb possessed more than the customary amount of self-assurance, resourcefulness, and a razor sharp mind. He had business instincts to match, and a spellbinding personality that would charm his way out of many an impossible predicament. There he was, a lad of 13, on his very first voyage, making enough tips from the ship's officers to venture his own bit of trading, i.e. a barrel of molasses and some boxes of fruit. These he parlayed into 20 silver dollars when he got back to Boston, which he then presented to his overjoyed Mother on his return to Brewster.

From then on Elijah Cobb, boy and man, broadened his experience on coasting trips to the West Indies and southern ports, graduating to be Master of the ship *Jane* when he was 24. She was loaded with flour and rice bound for Cadiz, and so far as Cobb was concerned his only worry on this voyage was Algerian pirates reported to be cruising the Gibraltar area. So he was mightily surprised when he was picked up by a French frigate and escorted into the French port of Brest. What Cobb had not reckoned on was the ferocity and chaos of the Reign of Terror in Revolutionary France, and what it could do to previously cordial American and French relationships.

Cobb writes, "Here commences my first trouble and anxiety as a ship Master – having under my charge a valuable vessel and cargo, inexperienced in business – carried into a foreign port, unacquainted with the language, no American consel, or merchant to advice with – and my reputation, as a ship master, depending on the measures I pursue."

Although his papers clearly indicate he was bound for Cadiz, a neutral port, the French prize-master who brought him in does not return them to Cobb. This limits his ability to do much of anything except watch his cargo of flour and rice vanish before the onslaught of the half-starved populace.

For six nerve-racking, frustrating weeks Cobb waits and waits. Finally word arrives that his case has been tried by the French court, although he was neither summoned to appear nor even informed of the action. The verdict . . . Cobb's ship is indeed neutral. He is to be paid for his cargo and receive demurrage (payment for each day of the detention of *Jane*, which continues to accrue for every day that passes until he actually has his money in hand). Cobb writes that the verdict of the court "gives a spring to my feelings." He feels better still when it is agreed, after 3 days of hard dickering, that he will be paid triple the cost of his cargo. Not only that, the French agent puts all this in writing. That is the good news.

**THE INDOMINITABLE
CAPTAIN ELIJAH COBB**

A commanding portrait study of loftiness
about to burst into laughter at itself!

The bad news is that under laws of the Revolution, no money can be carried out of the country. And the impoverished French have absolutely nothing to offer in trade goods.

Cobb is not one to believe in the adage "You can't get there from here." He agrees to accept bills of exchange payable by the French agent in Hamburg 60 days after he receives them. Time marches on and after a month of waiting he still has not received his bills. He sends the ship *Jane* home in ballast and prepares to take his case in person to Revolutionary headquarters in Paris.

With the whole of France in an uproar there is no public transportation; the best Cobb can hope for is the official dispatch coach. But it is absolutely forbidden to him or any other common citizen. However, Cobb turns on his never-failing charm and wins permission. He arms himself with pistols and a blunderbuss, anticipating the worst from countryside marauders, and boards the bullet-proofed coach. After three horrendous days and nights, where the least of his terrors are the dead bodies on the roadside, he arrives in Paris. And there bangs his head on Revolutionary stonewalling bureaucracy again.

Officials claim to have absolutely no knowledge about *Jane's* stolen cargo, or the promise of restitution. When Cobb gives them his written authorization that too disappears as had his ship's papers. Again Cobb turns on his wit and charm, thus ferreting out the information that he will do better if he takes his case to the top, to Robespierre in person, to rely on the Citizen Leader's especially friendly feelings toward America. Cobb goes back to his lodging and pens a letter:
"An American Citizen captured by a French Frigate on the high seas, requests a personal interview, and to lay his grievances before Citizen Roberspierre.

> Very respectfully
> E. Cobb."

Within an hour Cobb has his answer.

"I will grant Citizen Cobb an interview to morrow at 10AM.
Robespierre"

The interview goes well. Citizen R. tells Citizen C. to "see Citizen F.T." and tell him to produce the missing papers and finish Cobb's business immediately or F.T. will hear from Robespierre personally!

Cobb receives the promised bills of exchange, payable in 60 days. Being the sharp Brewster Yankee that he is, instead of accepting the bills on the spot he directs they be sent to him, care of the agent in Brest. He would make his transit thereto as leisurely as possible, letting the days tick by as the substantial demurrage payments piled up.

While Cobb was winning his battle, Robespierre was losing his. The man who made Cobb's success possible would shortly thereafter end his life on the guillotine.

Cobb's entire career would be one of challenges often even greater than his French experience. His ability to come out on the winning side brought his services as Shipmaster into great demand. He would run good New England rum into an Irish port when all foreign liquors were embargoed .. and come home with a pretty profit. On a trip to Hamburg his brig *Sally and Mary* would be seized by the British who had blockaded the port. Although the seizure would prove mostly bluff, Hamburg still remained off limits to him. But not for long. He would take his ship by inland canal, waters unguarded by the British, and slip into and out of Hamburg profitably, being further enriched by a growing knowledge of the devious ways of European trade in those days.

His ship *William Tell* would be seized by the British during the War of 1812. Briefly he would be their prisoner of war. Then Captain Cobb stayed home in Brewster throughout the rest of "Mr. Madison's War", so-called by local Captains put out of work by the event. It was in 1814, with the War still going on, that Cobb was

"MY PERTNER IN LIFES VOYAGE has run me in debt for a cape cod farm," wrote Elijah Cobb, while he was at sea. When he came home he liked it so much he took a year off to build the fine mansion still standing on Lower Road. It was completed in 1799, in time for a grand New Year's house warming celebration. But the Captain missed the party, for he was off to sea again. This photo was taken in 1897, nearly a century after Mrs. Cobb's open house party was the talk of the town.

chosen to be Moderator of one of Brewster's most notable September town meetings. The business of the day was British Captain Richard Ragett's threat to bombard Brewster's highly profitable salt works from his ship anchored offshore of them, unless he was paid $4,000 cash and no dillydallying. Cobb was selected for the job because of his notable business acumen and first-hand knowledge of dealing with the British. He had the additional qualification of being a Major in the local militia during the War.

Seated on the straight-backed, hard wooden pews, every bit as uncomfortable as the irksome money matter before them, the assemblage voted "to chuse a Committee of three persons to go through the town and take the value of the Saltworks, buildings and vessels – to assess the Sum of four thousand dollars" upon them. It must have exasperated Cobb considerably to find himself having to kowtow to the British when in times past he had so often outwitted them.

Raising $4,000 was easier said than done. Cape Codders in general, and Brewster Cape Codders in particular, were far too independent to comply easily when someone, a hated someone at that, demanded they fork over their hard-earned money. Besides, cold cash was an extremely scarce commodity back then. So as the hours ticked by and the deadline approached it looked very much as though Ragett would be bombarding the salt works. Finally, in desperation, Captain Clark, Selectman Thomas Seabury, and Elkanah Freeman personally made up the purse out of their own pockets. Local lore says they never got their money back. But it wasn't for lack of trying that reimbursment was not forthcoming.

In 1814 Brewster Selectmen petitioned the Legislature "to make good the doings of our Town Meeting held the 18th day of September." Again in 1815 they asked the Legislature "to refund the $.4000 paid Richard Ragett as a contribution". The Town was never reimbursed, but at least Clark, Freeman and Seabury were heroes for a time.

When the War of 1812 ended, Cobb went back to sea, making several voyages. Then in 1818 he embarked on a brand new venture, trade on the African coast, at Prince's Island. He loaded his ship *Ten Brothers* with cloth, tobacco, salt beef and other assorted trade goods and came back home with an exchange cargo of palm oil, gold dust, coffee and ivory. The voyage was so successful financially he could hardly wait to make a return trip. It was then that he urged his friends Captain Isaac Clark, his former First Mate now Captain David Nickerson, and Captain Joseph Mayo to join him. And it was then that the fabled Cobb luck ran out. The trip turned into a disaster of African fever and death, with 7 men and the 11-year-old cabin boy all dead.

In a desperate attempt to stem the progress of the fever, Cobb had *Ten Brothers* washed down with lime juice and vinegar, and fumigated for 24 hours with charcoal fires. But the fear was so strong of how much fever *Ten Brothers* might still harbor that, when she finally reached home, she was sunk at the end of the wharf where she was berthed.

Surely Shipmaster Elijah Cobb carried with him all the rest of his days the terrible grief and sense of responsibility for this disasterous trip. He never made another voyage. He retired to become a gentleman farmer on his Brewster lands, running northerly all the way to Cape Cod Bay from his fine home (which still stands on the curve of Lower Road) and stretching easterly to Breakwater Road. Never one to let enrichment pass by, he knew well the value of Breakwater Beach seaweed for manuring his fields. Today a crop of contemporary condominiums have sprung up on the Cobb land overlooking the pond that carries his name.

CAPSTAN

A vertical-cleated drum or cylinder revolving on an upright spindle. Used on shipboard for moving or raising heavy weights. Because of its traction power, the capstan is used to haul cables or anchor chains which could weigh hundreds of pounds.

Was the youngster he secreted aboard his ship truly the French Dauphin? The story of the Lost Dauphin is one told in many a seaport town in this country. This is how one Brewster Shipmaster would tell it.

SHIPMASTER DAVID NICKERSON 1772 – 1819

is an American in Paris during the French Revolution. There are food riots. Brutality, fear and an insane lack of accountability rule the country. The Royal Family has been imprisoned. Before it is all over Louis XVI and Marie Antoinette will lose their heads on the guillotine, to the cheering approval of the madding crowd. But what became of the Dauphin, the royal heir-to-be?

It is in such a setting that, to his astonishment, Capt. Nickerson is approached by a stranger, a woman who thrusts a child into his arms whispering that this is the Royal Prince, the Dauphin, France's hope. Save him . . . take him home to America . . . name him René Rousseau. Why that name? We have not a clue as to why, but then, the whole story seems a mystery.

Capt. Nickerson obeyed the woman's orders, brought René home, raised him as a son, taught him the ways of ships and seas, but in the end lost him to the sea when René was only 25. It was the close of a chapter with no sure beginnings and only questions at the end.

David Nickerson and Capt. Elijah Cobb must have been birds of a feather. Nickerson served as First Mate under Cobb. To satisfy a man of Cobb's demanding energy, Nickerson would have had to be very good at what he was doing. This was pretty well illustrated when Cobb, with Nickerson as his Mate, and his ship *Monsoon* loaded with good New England rum, delivered his cargo to a lucrative Hamburg market. Cobb then reloaded *Monsoon* with Russian and German goods, put Nickerson in charge and sent *Monsoon* home while Cobb would stay on in Hamburg negotiating another cargo, pending *Monsoon's* return several months later.

The fates of Nickerson and Cobb seem to have been inextricably connected, for better and for worse. Nickerson was in charge of the schooner *Hope* when he was approached by Cobb with a glowing story of his recent trip to Africa on *Ten Brothers*. The profits Cobb had reaped on a return cargo of gold and ivory, palm oil and coffee had been awesome. Cobb was getting up another trip and wanted to cut his special friends in on the get-rich-quick prospects of another African trading voyage. It probably did not take too much sell to fire Nickerson's spirit of adventure. He agreed to sign on *Ten Brothers* and was soon Africa bound.

The rest of the story is best told through Capt. Cobb's letters sent home from Prince's Island, Africa by a returning vessel.

On 4 Feb. 1819 Cobb wrote, "Capt. Nickerson is very sick on shore.

Feby 7th – Since the above, to the astonishment of all, Capt. Nickerson has so far recovered we have taken him on board.

Feby 14th – Nickerson does not gain any strength wishes to go to sea and try a change of air, he is sildom himself . . .

18th Feby – Capt. Nickerson is very sick on board this ship, but his fever being turned it was the advice of Every One to send him to sea, that a change of air would have good effect; I accordingly did, but I fear he will never reach America . . ."

Capt. Nickerson died at sea in 1819. His name, and that of his mystery son René Rousseau are inscribed together on one memorial stone in the Ancient Cemetery behind Brewster's First Parish Church. A stone not to mark the burial of mortal remains, but to cherish the memory of those lost at sea.

DEADEYE
A wooden block encircled by a rope or iron band and pierced with holes to receive a lanyard. Used especially to set up shrouds and stays.

THE BRIG

This was a trim 2-masted vessel having both fore and mainmast square rigged. The mainmast also carried a small fore-and-aft sail. The full-rigged *Brig* shown here was used largely for short trips and coastal trading. The *Brigantine*, a close cousin of the *Brig*, got its name from the fact that these maneuverable little vessels were favorites among Mediterranean brigands (pirates) who often equipped their vessels with oar power as well as sails. Another relative is the *Hermaphrodite Brig*, described on page 57.

Imagine the astonishment of the Russian people living in Arkhangelsk as they look out and see a ship flying the brand new American flag. Her Captain has brought his ship trading now that the American Revolutionary War is over, and American shippers, recuperating from the lingering economic disaster of war and embargoed ports, are carrying cargo again. The Captain would log his layover as the port of "Archangel."

SHIPMASTER ISAAC CLARK 1761 – 1819

is said to be the first American to sail into the White Sea, the first to visit Arkhangelsk. It is a frigid area, not far from the Arctic Circle. The name "White Sea" is an apt one for waters that are ice-bound a good part of the year.

Clark is used to trading in northern countries. Early on, when his fellow Brewster Shipmasters were taking their ships into more traditional moderate weather ports of France, Spain and South America, Clark was pioneering northward. In 1800 he had taken his ship *Financier* up into the icy waters of the Baltic Sea, through the Gulf of Finland and on to the Russian port of Kronshtadt. He had also gone trading at the Danish port of Elsinore. Thus he has a pretty good idea of what he is up against when he sets sail for what turns into his Arkhangelsk odyssey.

It begins when Clark comes sailing into the bitter cold waters of the White Sea to dock at the port of Arkangelsk, Russian territory which has just been opened to American trade. Would the frostbitten citizens appreciate the irony of a bark named *California* being their first American visitor?

When he goes ashore Clark learns that the newly appointed American Ambassador, who must give clearance for him to discharge cargo, has not yet arrived in Arkhangelsk, and may not arrive until who knows when. Clark hopefully waits and waits. And then, fearing impending winter will lock his ship in the ice, he waits no longer.

FRAMED WITH RUSSIAN FIR brought back from Archangel by Captain Isaac Clark, his fine home is still occupied by family. It was here in 1803, in Captain Clark's parlor, on the Captain's handsome mahogany desk, (now on display at the Brewster Historical Society Museum) that official papers were signed which formally separated the North Parish of Harwich from the South Parish, thus creating the Town of Brewster. Curiously, these nearly 200 year-old documents, drawn up at a time when women had no franchise, contain the signature of one woman, Marcy Clark, wife of one Kimball Clark.

You might call Clark the ultimate do-it-yourself Shipmaster, for what he does next is astonishing. He hires a sledge, a type of heavy-duty Russian sleigh, and makes a dash to St. Petersburg to call upon the American Ambassador who, it seems, prefers the social season there to the winter wilds of Arkangelsk. Having thus obtained the necessary clearance papers, Clark dashes back to *California*, unloads her cargo, reloads with good Russian fir timber, then heads back home. The timber will be used to build his new Georgian style mansion on Stony Brook Road in Brewster.

As a retiree, Clark soon found himself facing the reefs and dangers of navigating the intricate channels of politics, as Brewster's elected Representative to the General Court. Here he served from 1803 to 1812. Then, sometime in 1819, friend and neighbor Captain Elijah Cobb would drop by to urge Clark to join him in an African venture. Cobb had recently returned from a trip to Africa, aboard his ship *Ten Brothers*, and had brought back a hugely profitable cargo of palm oil, gold dust, ivory, and coffee. He urged Clark to join him in a second trip to Africa. Clark demurred. But finally, with reluctance, he was persuaded and agreed to sign on. Did Clark perhaps have an uneasy premonition of the disaster that would befall *Ten Brothers* . . . of the ferocity of Africa's Black Water Fever . . . crew and officers sick, dead, dying . . . and Clark among them, buried on Africa's Prince's Island so far from Brewster and Arkhangelsk.

SHIP'S
WHEEL

The maiden voyage of any vessel was an event, and still is. But the maiden voyage of a clipper ship, now that was another story . . . a mighty test of man vs. ship to see what she could and would do, and who was going to be the boss. Learning the tricks of these wild new flyers took nerves of steel, and a form of ship-smarts Kittredge describes as a mixture of intuition and the gift of prophecy.

SHIPMASTER TULLY CROSBY 1809 – 1891

drove two great clippers on their maiden voyages, winning for himself and his ships well-earned fame. Like so many Shipmasters his career began humbly enough . . . a 13 year-old signed up as cabin boy with his brother Capt. Joshua Crosby. He sailed under his brother for 10 years. Then at 23 he became Captain of the brig *Old Colony*, then went on to the bark *Arab*, and the ships *Charlotte* and *Monterey*.

Then in 1851 he became Master of the brand new ship *Antelope*. He took her half way 'round the world from Boston to Frisco, then on to Shanghai, then back across the Pacific, around the Horn, bringing *Antelope* smartly into New York Harbor. So successful was this trip that 2 years later Crosby was assigned command of the beautiful new clipper ship *Kingfisher*. Hardly off the ways, *Kingfisher* was immediately challenged by Donald McKay's great clipper *Bald Eagle*, to a sprint for San Francisco.

On the first day of October, 1853, *Bald Eagle* weighs anchor and clears Boston Harbor. But *Kingfisher* is delayed for two hectic, long days before she can take chase. Crosby is pushing his ship to the limit trying to make up lost time, and he has almost made it. Then just off Frisco the wind dies, fog rolls in and *Kingfisher* is becalmed for 5 bitter days. But then the fog lifts and the two great clipper ships come sweeping through the Golden Gate almost within hailing distance of one another. If the sight of today's Tall Ships sets your heart thumping, picture yourself standing on the sunny, windswept shores of Frisco Bay, watching two of the world's most beautiful ships come charging in, a "bone in their teeth" and every inch of sail set.

Capt. Crosby brought *Kingfisher* home to New York Harbor, then retired in a blaze of glory. Perhaps he felt this had been the greatest challenge of his career, and most assuredly anything else would be an anti-climax.

Crosby spent the rest of his life in Brewster, serving his town at various times as Representative to the General Court. He must have met a number of retired Cape Cod Shipmasters there, for many were similarly elected. Those must have been thunderous and salty sessions!

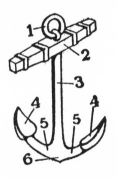

ANCHOR
1. Ring
2. Wooden Stock
3. Shank
4. Flukes
5. Arms
6. Crown

The town might well have been named Dillingham instead of Brewster. After all, John Dillingham was one of the first to settle this territory, removing himself and his family from Quaker constraints in well-established Sandwich for the freedom of a new frontier in the wilderness of Satucket, as the Indians called what is now Brewster. He settled on a land grant that ran clear across the Cape from Bay to Ocean.

Here in 1661 he built the family homestead, a firm, upright saltbox structure of many assorted windows, its front door close onto the sandy path which would become the Old King's Highway – Rte. 6A. There it still stands today, telling something of the integrity of the builder. Two centuries later the Dillingham independence and self-confidence would give spirit to his descendant

SHIPMASTER JAMES DILLINGHAM 1831 – 1883

It is 1863 and the Civil War is in progress on land and at sea. Commanding the fine old clipper *Snow Squall*, Dillingham is returning from a journey to Penang. He has rounded the Cape of Good Hope and is well into the Atlantic on the last leg of his journey when he sights the auxiliary bark *Tuscaloosa*. (Auxiliary means she has the advantage of both sail and steam power.) *Tuscaloosa* comes along within hailing distance, with her Stars and Stripes flying, in response to Dillingham's flag.

Then suddenly *Tuscaloosa's* gun ports fly open, up goes the Confederate flag, and Dillingham is ordered to heave to. Dillingham signifies assent, but keeps working *Squall* as if inept at managing her. By the time the Confederate Captain realizes it is not poor seamanship that separates the two, Dillingham is well out of range, distancing *Squall* so far from *Tuscaloosa* that not even the Confederate's cannon shots can reach her. *Tuscaloosa* pursues well into the evening. But despite her advantage of having steam power, she proves no match for Dillingham's skillful maneuvering of *Squall*.

Dillingham brought *Snow Squall* into New York and was there rewarded by her underwriters with a purse of $1,375.14. Undoubtedly this was more useful to him, even with the odd change, than the customary silver tea service. It was rare indeed when a Union sailing vessel eluded an auxiliary powered Confederate. But then, Brewster Shipmasters were a rare lot.

THE HOUSE THAT DILLINGHAM INDEPENDENCE BUILT in 1661, when John Dillingham abandoned the orderd life of Sandwich for freedom in the wilderness of Satucket (now Brewster). With such an ancestral background it is no wonder that some 200 years later Shipmaster James Dillingham, aboard *Snow Squall*, would demonstrate great ingenuity and self-confidence in escaping capture by a Confederate vessel. Nine generations of Dillinghams lived in the house, possibly the oldest in Brewster.

Everyone in town was well aware of his success and prosperity, for he had just built a fine new 10-room home in the very center of Brewster . . . where Parson Simpkin's ancient four-square parsonage had stood, and where the preacher had written his 1806 *Topographical Description of Brewster* (which tells us, among other interesting things, that Brewster folk were so short of firewood that they were learning to burn peat). The grand new mansion on Breakwater Road reflected the wealth and status, in 1862, of

SHIPMASTER WILLIAM FREEMAN 1820 – 1905

He had cargoed lumber for his new home on one of his trips to Alaska. When in France he ordered Aubusson carpets. The hall floor was laid after the handsome new "barber pole" style, alternating narrow floor boards of creamy white maple and rich, dark mahogany. Captain Freeman was 42 at this triumphal time in his life. When a man began his career as a Shipmaster at nineteen, twenty or twenty-two, 42 was an advanced age. Maybe Freeman would have stayed home for good, to enjoy his fine home and his prominence in town, had he but known the future he would face when he was commissioned to take command of *Mogul*.

Mogul was a top of the line ship, built for the Sears Company by master shipwrights of Kennebunk, Maine. Captain Freeman would take her over in a series of more or less routine trans-Atlantic runs, and then go trading on *Mogul* in South America, and the Far East.

She had done well on her last trip from Cardiff, Wales to Rio de Janiero, to Akyab, Burma, and back to Hamburg. Then, on April 24, 1874, *Mogul* sails from Liverpool loaded with coal destined for San Francisco. She is some 93 days out when Freeman is informed that *Mogul's* cargo of coal is on fire. (One wonders why every shipload of coal didn't burn considering that a wet hold filled with tons of coal is a formula for spontaneous combustion.) For 5 days, 24-hours a day, the crew fights the fire, all the while sailing desperately onward in the hope of making Honolulu. Captain Freeman makes every preparation for abandoning ship, but holds off the order as long as *Mogul* can be managed. He is only too well aware that at any moment the fire could flash into an inferno.

For another horrifying week the battle continues. Then, with all hope gone, on August 7 the entire crew of twenty-seven men take to the open boats. Ahead of them lie 1,200 miles of open ocean before the Marquesas Islands will show on the horizon. Capt. Freeman's boat makes land first. For the next worry-filled days Freeman watches and waits as one by one the rest of the lifeboats straggle in, the men exhausted and burned by salt and sun. Then luck smiles on them. A trading schooner heading for San Francisco takes the lot aboard. Four long months after abandoning *Mogul* at sea they disembark on the shores of the good old USA. "On arrival they were looked on as having risen from the dead," wrote one observer. (A curious and somber note: Capt. Freeman was still in San Francisco awaiting passage home to Brewster, and had been there for two weeks, when news of the burning of *Centaur* arrived, informing him of the loss of his friend and neighbor Capt. Nathan Foster, whose story is told next).

Capt. Freeman would go on to sail one of the most unusual ships with which he, or any other Master, would be involved. She was a square-rigged 4-masted bark named *Ocean King*, the largest sailing vessel afloat at that time with the exception of a tremendous great 4-master built by Donald McKay. *Ocean King* would also be lost at sea, but that was another chapter, under a different Master, five years later.

Capt. Freeman long ago sailed on; he was a hale 86 years old when J. Henry Sears wrote about him in his famous book about *Shipmasters of Brewster*. The fine home, boasting a barber pole floor, still stands as the Freeman Inn welcoming travelers from far and wide.

IT SEEMS A BIT ECCENTRIC, at least today. Another member of the Freeman family, Shipmaster Solomon Freeman, bought the steeple from the First Parish Church, paying $1.05 for it when, in 1852, renovations were being made. Could he possibly have sailed it off somewhere to a new, and as yet undiscovered, used-church- steeple market?

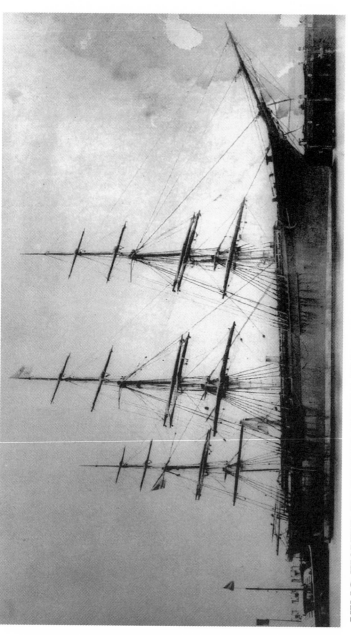

KING FISHER IN HONG KONG HARBOR

King Fisher's career was not always as somber as portrayed in this picture of her last Hong Kong visit under Shipmaster William Freeman. Her maiden voyage was a wild race to Frisco against speed champion *Bald Eagle*. Although *Eagle* got a two day start, the two clippers came flying through the Golden Gate in a 'sprit to 'sprit finish.
Note paddle wheel steamer, left background . . . an omen of things to come.

The ship's sailing card portrays a colorful New York dockside scene with the *W.B. Dinsmore* sleek and trim alongside, and draft horses hauling a huge load of Frisco-bound freight. It advertises "Merchant's Express Line of Clipper Ships for San Francisco – dispatching only those standing in the first class in all respects. The splendid A1 clipper ship *W. B. Dinsmore*".

SHIPMASTER NATHAN FOSTER 1833 – 1874

Foster had the experience to handle such a fine ship. At the advanced sea-going age of 23 he had commanded the medium clipper *Expounder* on her maiden voyage. It is said that the name *Expounder* was inspired by the fiery oratory of Daniel Webster, then at the height of popular esteem, and known as the "Defender of the Constitution and Expounder of the same". Foster headed *Expounder* out of her home port Boston for Cardiff, Wales, and thence to San Francisco. From there he would work her on her way home via Callao, Peru (of guano fame) and then to Baltimore.

Foster had the misfortune to be in command of *W.B. Dinsmore* on a passage from Liverpool to San Francisco when she took fire by spontaneous combustion in her cargo of coal. Although this great ship was lost, all hands were rescued by an English vessel. The *Dinsmore's* bones may rest eternally at the bottom of the ocean, but her memory still sails proudly in the front parlor of the Brewster Ladies' Library, where her ship portrait hangs, a gift of J. Henry Sears in 1899.

Not one to sit at home and twiddle his thumbs when things were quiet, Capt. Foster occasionally did some coast trading aboard the sloop *Morning Star*, a not unusual pursuit for Shipmasters between ocean-going assignments.

Capt. Foster was to face the horror of fire at sea a second time while in charge of the ship *Centaur*. The year was 1874, and the story is told in the diary of Capt. William Freeman who himself had just survived such an ordeal on his ship *Mogul*.

Wrote Freeman, "This morning the brig *Nautilus* arrived in San Francisco via the Marquesas, and on board are the second mate and four seamen from the *Centaur*, who bring the sad intelligence that she is also burned and worse that all the rest, that Capt. Foster with boat and crew are lost. The statement of the second officer and men is that they took to the boats on the evening of the 18th Aug., and lay by the ship through the night, and that the *Centaur* went down about 3 AM on the 19th. In the morning the first mate's boat was not to be seen. The Capt. and second mate then shaped their course (in separate boats) for the Marquesas and kept company until the morning of the 23rd, when at about 3 AM they saw the Capt.'s boat capsize, but the wind blowing strong and much sea they couldn't render them assistance."

Of the 38 Captain's named in "Shipmasters of the First Parish Church" 8 are listed as lost at sea and 4 died in foreign ports. Although this sampling is small, it suggests that being a Shipmaster entailed a high risk that the Captain's wife would become a widow. This daunting thought seems not at all to have deterred Brewster men from going off to sea.

THE PACIFIC OCEAN measures some 64,186,300 square miles of El Niño, La Niña and La Mama weather breeding and typhoon propagating expanse. The Atlantic, at 13,429,000 square miles is noted, among other hazards, for Bermuda Triangle disappearing acts, Sargosso Sea doldrums, and havoc-wreaking hurricanes. Those are surface miles only, and do not reckon the depths in cold fathoms that claimed so many Brewster men.

By some folks' rules, one is only a true Cape Codder when the family archives trace back to the Mayflower, or thereabouts. But

SHIPMASTER ALLEN S. BRAGG 1874 – 1956

became a genuine Cape Codder in an initiation that few, if any, Brewster-born folks had undergone, and lived to tell the tale. He was born on Ocracoke Island off North Carolina. This is where the notorious pirate captain Black Beard finally met his demise aboard his ship *Adventure*. She was being pursued one fateful day in 1718 by two British sloops, and in Ocracoke Inlet pirates and pursuers came together in a roaring fight of broadsides and clashing swords. Black Beard took on British Lieutenant Robert Maynard sword-to-sword. And in the horrendous combat that ensued, Black Beard was stabbed and shot but still fought on . . . until one great slash of a sword decapitated him. The *Adventure* is believed to still lie on the bottom of the Inlet.

Brought up in the bedazzlement of such local lore, and the challenge to live up to it, it was not surprising that Bragg had earned his navigator's license by age 18, and was Master of his own vessel. She went under the name of *Mary A. Tyler*. Bragg was so able an entrepreneur that he ran his own business coasting along the Eastern seaboard, with occasional crossings to European ports.

Coasting is what he was doing on November 17, 1898, when he was caught up in a holy terror of a gale in Cape Cod Bay. Howling winds catch *Mary* and swing her totally out of control. Monster waves claw her into shallow water and onto the Brewster flats at Paine's Creek, there to pound her to pieces. While *Mary A. Tyler* did not survive this gale, remarkably Captain Bragg did.

You would not have read much about *Mary's* fate in the newspapers because the big news then was all about the terrible disastrous sinking of the steamship *Portland*, somewhere off Provincetown, with 157 lives lost, and drowned bodies washing up on Cape Cod shores.

This was hardly the best introduction to Brewster, but Captain Bragg later found Brewster so agreeable that he married here and started a Bragg family dynasty. The Captain served in WWI as a Navy officer, crossing the Atlantic on troop transports. Even with the hazards of war, this part of his career must have seemed relatively tame to a man who, in the truest sense, became a Cape Cod wash-ashore in the Great Portland Gale.

CHOCK

A heavy casting of metal, or piece of wood, shaped with short, upward-curved arms between which ropes or hawsers are passed for towing, mooring, etc. Its purpose is to hold lines in position and to protect surrounding surfaces from abrasion.

THE EVENING NEWS covering the latest disaster at sea, or the death of a Brewster Shipmaster in a foreign port, could be several months in arriving. There was no working trans-Atlantic cable to spread the word until 1866. Not until 1878 were there telephones, and then only a limited number where phone lines were strung. No wires, no message. This also applied to the early telegraph which was totally dependent upon wire connections; wireless telegraphy was not invented until 1874. The driving of the Golden Spike, signalling the final spanning of the continent by railroad lines, didn't take place until 1869. So there was a great disconnection when a man shipped out. What trickle of news there was would be contained in personally delivered messages, or in letters handed from one Brewster Shipmaster to another homeward bound. Imagine the waiting, the not knowing. We complain nowadays of information overkill. But think how much worse it was then to have no information at all!

"As though hurricanes, fevers and land sharks (unscrupulous business types) were not enough to try the mettle of Yankee Captains, in the Caribbean pirates infested these waters as well," says Henry Kittredge, author of the definitive work on Cape Cod Shipmasters. One person who could tell you first-hand about pirates was

SHIPMASTER WARREN LINCOLN 1810 – 1900

He met his first pirate at the age of 12. He was cabin boy for Brewster Capt. Freeman Mayo, aboard the brig *Iris*. *Iris* was sailing in Caribbean waters when Mayo sighted a pirate vessel a short distance away. There was no escape for *Iris*, she was becalmed. The pirates, on the other hand, had both sails and oars, and used their long sweeps so effectively they were soon alongside and clambering aboard.

Young Lincoln saw the pirates ransack the ship. He saw their leader come back up on deck attired in Capt. Mayo's best shore-going clothes. Lincoln heard the pirates demand that Mayo produce money, and plenty of it if he and his crew, and that included young Lincoln, wanted to live. He heard Mayo answer that he had very little money aboard but could raise some if the pirates would take him to Mantanzas, in Cuba, about 30 miles distant. Taking Mayo at his word, the pirates worked *Iris* into a small bay where their headquarters were located, and then delivered Mayo to Matanzas.

It proved far from easy for Mayo to raise the money; there seemed to be considerable indifference as to the fate of *Iris*, her crew or Captain. Mayo had almost given up hope when to his wonderment appeared the US naval vessel *Alligator* sailing smartly into port. Upon hearing Mayo's story, her Captain had Mayo pilot *Alligator* to the pirate cove where *Iris* lay. There was a sharp fight. When the pirates, or what was left of them, fled, Mayo had himself put on board *Iris*. There to his horror he found every last soul gone, man and boy.

Now for the story through young Warren Lincoln's eyes. With a sinking heart he watches Capt. Mayo take off with some of the pirates on his ransom raising mission. Those feelings are shared by all the crew, but despite their concerns they are especially careful not to show their feelings or to aggravate their captors. Behind this impassive front, however, there are secret signals, quiet whispers. The crew tells Lincoln they are going to make a break for it. The signal comes, there's a sharp scuffle. Most everyone suffers cuts and bruises, but they all do escape, piling into one of the boats and rowing for their lives. Then it becomes a game of hide-and-seek. They keep their boat in close to shore to avoid being sighted by the pirates. There's an irony in that fact. For it just could be that while they are thus hidden, *USS Alligator* sweeps by with Capt. Mayo aboard on a rescue mission to save *Iris* and her crew.

To young Lincoln it seems like they will never get there, but finally they do make port at Matanzas. While their wounds are being dressed they learn that Capt. Mayo has gone aboard *Alligator* in a rescue mission. Along with the pain of their cuts and bruises there is a lot of worry about what is going to happen to them now.

Then . . . here comes *Iris* sailing into Matanzas, crewed by some of *Alligator's* men, with Capt. Mayo in command. Young Lincoln whoops a cheer!

Back on board *Iris*, Lincoln, the crew and Capt. Mayo square away for Charleston, where the Captain buys a cutlass and musket for each man. His encounter with pirates didn't scare Warren Lincoln away from the sea. He would later Captain the brig *Draco* and the bark *Mary*, but retired when he was only 35 because of poor health. Around 1850 he started a general store. The building still stands, now a private home located on Route 6A in Brewster, overlooking School House Pond. An 1895 Town Report shows the Town paid storekeeper Warren Lincoln $14.50 for providing a few supplies to the poor house, and another $4.85 for school items. The Brewster Historical Society has a picture of the old Shipmaster standing in front of his store. He wears a vast beard that could easily make him take sail on a high wind. Perhaps retiring from the hazards of piracy was all Capt. Lincoln needed to restore his health, for he lived to be 90 years old.

RETIRED SHIPMASTER WARREN LINCOLN

sorted mail and dispensed groceries in his store, and found time to record some of Brewster's more colorful happenings. Such as the occasion when Brewster's Artillery Company, in the course of training exercises, loaded up and fired their cannon, but it failed to discharge. Moments pass. Nothing happens. There is much discussion. Then suddenly, just as a careless lad walks by, there's a great VROOM! Horrified Company members rush the lad to the house across the way, sure he is dying. There's dreadful suspense ... awful waiting among onlookers. Then the lad reappears, hale and whole again, except for his shot-off coat tails.

His ship *Katahdin* still sails on in a perpetually raging sea, her sails furled all except for one jib, smoke streaking from her auxiliary engine, as she strains against the gale. Adding to the wild scene, in the background a sinking ship rolls on her beam ends.

SHIPMASTER ISAAC WEATHERBEE 1836 – 1875

Master if the *Katahdin* at age 24, he may have dictated to the artist how he wished his ship portrayed. It would be hung over the parlor mantle at home to help keep his family in mind of his doings. And remind all viewers of his mastery of such a situation. But such a picture would likely bring little comfort to the family on stormy nights, with the Captain far away, who-knows-where at sea.

In 1868, Capt. Isaac Weatherbee inherited the family home on Breakwater Road, a tall, narrow house overlooking the beach scene where the Brewster packet ships had been so active. Here his seagoing lap desk, his Bowditch *Practical Navigator,* a few pieces of exquisite Rose Medallion porcelain, and a pair of Celadon jardinieres suggest that business called him to far ports, though not necessarily on *Katahdin.*

For *Katahdin* was a small vessel of only 548 tons, according to Lloyd's American Register. She was of down Maine Yankee shipwright workmanship, built in 1847, sold in '63 in Bordeaux, France. And there lost her New England identity to a new name, spelled "Cosair" in the records.

Capt. Weatherbee would also end his Shipmaster's career far from home. He died in San Francisco, possibly from one of the fevers which periodically swept through that seaport town. While his earthly remains lie in San Francisco, his name appears on a stone in the Lower Road Cemetery, reminding the Sea Captains Town that he too was a Brewster Shipmaster.

KATAHDIN TRIUMPHING OVER ADVERSITY

Like many ship portraits, this one of *Katahdin* is filled with symbolism. Depicted with her bow to the right means Katahdin is leaving port. (Bow pointed left would indicate a ship arriving.) *Katahdin* is bound to triumph over the horrendous storm for she sails toward the promise of brightening skies. While ships in the background wallow in terrible distress, *Katahdin* rides high, her bow cutting proudly through the waves, clearly indicating her superiority over others, for she has the latest auxiliary steam power. And as a final emblem of *Katahdin's* command over all situations, her hull is painted black much like a man-of-war, with white stripe and black gunports. With such impressive presence how would pirates know they weren't real?

He himself may not have been famous in the annals of the sea. But his ship *Expounder* has a place of unabridged glory; her portrait hangs in the White House Naval Mess!

SHIPMASTER ROBERT IRVINE 1835 – 1895

Expounder came under his command when Irvine was a well-seasoned Master 36 years old, and she but a young maiden of 15. Classified as a medium clipper, built more for cargo than speed, she was 171' long, constructed of rock-hard oak, drew 23' of water and had a beam of 37', statistics that give you an idea of the size of many of the medium clippers.

Irvine was following in some mighty footsteps when he took her over. Capt. Nathan Foster had put *Expounder* through her paces on her first voyage in 1856. None other than Josiah Nickerson Knowles took her around the Horn to Frisco three years later.

Irvine took command in 1871 when time was already running out on delivering the goods by sail. Only 22 years after she slid down the ways in all her glorious clippership beauty, *Expounder* was stripped of her rigging and became a barge. Such conversions were to become commonplace when steam-produced horsepower, rather than windpower, drove more and more ships more and more economically. *Expounder* finally disappeared from the ships register in 1906. It was a long career for a wooden ship. She had outlived Capt. Irvine and the other great Shipmasters who commanded her.

Possibly Irvine's lack of strong identity hereabouts lies not in a lack of luster in his career, but in the fact that he did what Cape Codders would consider the unthinkable. He moved from Brewster to Texas. And there he made his living working a lighter, loading and off-loading vessels moored in deep water rather than dockside. Probably, as a lad, Irvine had watched the loading and unloading of Brewster packets; he would have known all about the intricacies of this type of Shipmastering.

It would appear that one Brewster Captain went native!

SHIPMASTER JOHN HIGGINS – Dates Unknown

He earned the title of Captain when he sailed the 50-foot sloop *Morning Star* (the same vessel Capt. Nathan Foster occasionally took over) coasting in and out of nearby ports, making and trading cargo. But the lure of California gold fields caught up with Higgins. To make passage, he embarked as a crewman on the *Albatross* when Brewster Capt. Winslow Knowles sailed out to San Francisco. However, having gotten that far, Higgins felt there was a still brighter future awaiting him in the Australian gold fields. That led him to embark on a steamer headed for Down Under, which shipwrecked on the way.

Were this not so, Higgins might have met up, in Australia, with a Brewster neighbor named Freeman Cobb. A true chip off his grandfather Elijah Cobb's block, Freeman realized the entrepreneurial possibilities of Australia's gold fields, and that they could only be fully exploited if there was a transportation system to serve them. So Freeman Cobb imported a sample of the fabled, horse-drawn Concord Coach which had been most successful transporting passengers and goods over New England's badly rutted roads. He adapted the coach to the even more dreadful road conditions in Australia at that time, and thereby opened up new routes to accommodate gold fever traffic. Thus a transportation system was devised that would change the course of Australia's history and economic development. Even today in Australia the name of Cobb & Co. is revered. Freeman Cobb, while not a Brewster Shipmaster, had the enterprising spirit of those who were.

Now back to Higgins. He managed to survive the steamer's sinking, and after drying himself out he shipped as Second Mate on a trading brig. It was not unusual in those days for a man to be Master on one ship and Mate on another, depending on the opportunities of the trip and the requirements of those doing the hiring. He was well fitted for the job, knew the business well from his days in charge of *Morning Star*. But apparently he brought aboard a jinx, for this brig was also wrecked. When Higgins, half drowned, washed ashore on one of the Caroline Islands inhabited by a few natives they welcomed him. He in turn, like any good Yankee business man, soon had the people carrying on a profitable trade in coconut oil, hogs and tortoise shell with crews of visiting whaling ships.

To prove how small the Brewster Shipmasters had made the world, whaling Capt. Charles Freeman came ashore one day, planning a few hours of trading, and stayed with Higgins for a week, gathering all kinds of information to bring back home to Brewster about John Higgins, his business ventures, his success in Christianizing the island people, and about the native woman who became Mrs. Higgins.

Higgins' paradise would come to an end about ten years after it began, when natives from another island came ashore, got into a scrap, and Higgins was stabbed to death. Capt. John Higgins' story proved to many a Brewster lad that romantic dreams of adventure and tropical islands could come true. At least for a while.

ACTUALLY SHE WAS A BLONDE no matter what that Chinese portrait of her says. Eliza Emma Winslow Foster, wife to Brewster Shipmaster Francis Baily Foster. It was on one of his trips to China that Capt. Foster commissioned a local artist to paint his wife's portrait, not from the lady herself, but from a tintype image. That was when Eliza Emma Winslow Foster became a handsome brunette. Look at her portrait in the Brewster Historical Society Museum and imagine which way you would like her best.

THE HALF & HALF
HERMAPHRODITE BRIG

What else would you call a vessel with a front half sporting the tried and true rigging of a brig . . . and aft of pure schooner conformation? Undoubtedly the first Hermaphrodite to come off the ways caused a spate of doubtful speculation and derisive hoots from beholders eyeing her ambiguous appearance.

However, as was true in many other commercial endeavors, innovation in design was what kept the ship building business exciting and profitable, both for designers and the ultimate owners who were always looking for faster, cheaper, less labor-intensive ways to transport passengers and freight. And wanted it all in the latest model.

NAUTICALLY SPEAKING:

One knot = 1 mile
One US Nautical Mile = 6080.20 feet
One Route 6 mile = 5280 feet

It is one of those curious facts that land miles and sea miles aren't the same length. Curiouser still, that sea miles per hour are measured in knots.

Although a seeming anomaly nowadays, the knot was a pretty ingenious concept back when clocks were a rarity. Those early clocks that did exist were more curiosities and ornaments than reliable time keepers. The average clock would lose 15 or more minutes a day. So there was no accurate way to time how fast a ship was traveling, or how far it had gone in a period of time. That's where knots came in. They helped determine how fast the ship was sailing, and how much watery longitude it had covered. More or less. But "more or less" made sea travel pretty risky business. Over the centuries thousands of ships and their crews have rocked in the cradle of the deep because there was no good way to figure the longitudinal position on the ship.

Determining latitude, or how far north or south the vessel was located, posed no problem. Way back, Greek astronomers had figured out those horizontal lines you see on maps, running parallel to the Equator. Copying the Greeks, sailors could easily calculate latitude by "shooting" the sun or stars, providing it wasn't cloudy. But calculating longitude (those imaginary lines spaces 15° apart that run from pole to pole) without an accurate timekeeper was impossible. Until someone thought of knots.

A seaman paid out a rope into the wake of the ship. The rope was tied with knots at regular, pre-measured intervals. As each knot slipped through the seaman's hands, drawn out by the passage of the ship through the water, a second seaman kept his eye on an hourglass, or sandglass as they were then known. If 5 knots moved through the seaman's hands in 60 sandglass minutes, then the ship was traveling 5 knots per hour.

Until the mid-1700s no one had discovered how to make an accurate clock, though it was not for trying! Even as newer and better clocks were designed and downsized to fit aboard a cramped-for-space ship, they were still useless at sea. For the ship's motion, the humidity, and changes in temperature severely affected the accuracy of any 18th century clock.

In fact, sailors were still depending on knots right up until 1761 (the same year Brewster's great Shipmaster Isaac Clark was born) when a truly seaworthy chronometer went to sea for the first time. On a $6^1/2$ week test run, sailing from Britain to Jamaica, it lost only 5 seconds. Phenomenal!

No, the chronometer didn't put a stop to the wrecks and losses at sea. But it had to help reduce them substantially. And, at the least, the Captain would have a fair idea where he was when his ship went down!

In the days of clipper ships, and up to the mid- and late 1800s, Brewster Shipmasters in particular were renowned among their peers for their exceptional abilities. In a large part this seems to be the result of a genetic predisposition to supreme self-confidence, added to unbounded Cape Cod Yankee ingenuity, with a high quotient of a unique Brewster brand of perspicacity blended in. With the arrival of the chronometer, Brewster sea men had all they needed to voyage anywhere and everywhere, to ports that had never before seen a Cape Cod man. They knew who they were, and how to get there from here. A sure formula for greatness.

Today, with scientists sailing ships into outer space, Cesium atomic clocks keep the time, so accurately that it is claimed these clocks will lose only 1 second in 1.4 million years. And when the next generation of super timekeepers comes off the drawing board in the not too distant future, it is predicted they will be accurate to within 1 second in 313 million years. All of which doesn't stop today's sailors of the seas from still recording in ships' logs their travels measured in knots.

Definition: *Clipper Ship* – a vessel with a bowsprit, 3 masts (each with a topgallant mast) – square rigged on all 3 masts. Clippers were so-called because they "clipped through" the waves rather than thrusting through them as did other types of vessels.

RARELY HAS THERE BEEN A MORE BEAUTIFUL SIGHT AT SEA than a clipper ship winging her way across the ocean, seemingly perfectly attuned to wind, waves and sky. Clippers represented the crowning glory of the age of sail. First launched in 1850 by the famous ship designer Donald McKay, they were the ultimate answer, in their day, to the unrelenting quest for speed and more speed. But for all their unmatched glory, and their owners' understandable pride in these sleek, swift vessels, clippers were to fade from the scene less than two decades after their first launching, victims of their excessive specialization. For they were built for speed at the sacrifice of cargo space.

With demand growing for greater and greater shipping capacity to satisfy burgeoning world trade, the lean, fast "extreme clippers" as they were called, gave way to slower, wider ships, rather nostalgically called "medium clippers". These clippers measured their triumphs of passage not by setting speed records, but by transporting record-breaking tonnage.

When, in the early 1850s, Shipmaster J. Henry Sears commanded the clipper *Titan* she was one of the fasted ships of her day. And Sears set a talk-of-the-trade record freighting 6,900 bales of cotton from southern ports to Liverpool, in very good time. Only 20 years later one of the new breed of cargo carriers would surpass *Titan's* cargo record by carrying 19,000 bales. A far less elegant passage, for sure, but a far more profitable venture.

Even while these record-breaking statistics were the shipping news of the day, the era of merchant marine under sail was already inexorably facing extinction. The course of its downfall was foreshadowed by black smoke belching from the funnels of the first experimental steam-powered ship launched in 1818. By the 1870s

steam-powered cargo vessels would dominate the fleet, in swift-
ness of trip and in cargo capacity. For they would plod out to sea to
make their ports of call in weeks rather than months required by
sailing vessels, dependent as they were on the vagaries of wind and
weather.

But even this new way of getting things there faster would more
than meet its match in the railroads. By 1869 if you wanted to ship
something to Frisco from Boston or New York, both you and it
could be there in a few days by rail . . . where voyages under sail
would take 3 or more months, and by steam, several weeks.

Gone was the era of wooden ships and iron men. Rare, from then
on, the Brewster lad who started his training in Shipmastering as a
cabin boy, age 12.

U NDENIABLE AS THE BEAUTY OF THE CLIPPER
SHIPS WAS, for the sailors who worked them, life aboard a
clipper was about as hard as life could get. The labor involved in
taking a clipper from here to there is absolutely beyond our ken
today. Just for starters, in sailing the shortest route between two
points is rarely a straight line. In order to make the most of available wind power, from whatever angle it blew, the clipper had to
be tacked, zigzagging across its course. Thus a trip of 3,000 miles as
the crow flies might become 5,000 miles or more as the clipper
sailed. Every time the tack had to be altered the crew had to haul
around yards that could weigh tons. And should stormy winds
threaten to shred the canvas, be it day or pitch black night, up
into the rigging struggled the crew to reef or strike sails. Think of
it . . . the ship swaying, and the higher you get the more you feel it.
The gale tears at you. It may be raining furiously. Or snow ices up
the rigging. It won't happen just once or twice a trip, but time after
time, fair weather or foul. There's no choice . . . up you go!

WILD RANGER – Launched 1853

Shipmaster J. Henry Sears took charge of *Wild Ranger* on her 1853 maiden voyage. Sears was then only 24 years old. He remained in command during her first two years plying between Boston and San Francisco, a burgeoning new settlers market which had boomed following the discovery of gold in 1848.

The astonishing account of the wreck of the *Wild Wave*, and the subsequent adventures of her Captain and crew, are related in the diary of

CAPTAIN JOSIAH NICKERSON KNOWLES 1830 – 1896

"March 5th, 1858 – At 1 AM, the ship at the time going at the rate of 13 knots per hour, to our great astonishment and alarm the lookout reported breakers under the lea. So close was our proximity to the rocks and so great our speed, that it was impossible to avoid running upon them, and in less than five minutes the good ship *Wild Wave* was on a coral reef, full of water, and the seas breaking over her, Our masts were snapping and cracking at a fearful rate. The excitement among the passengers and crew was intense. It being very dark we were unable to determine whether we were near land or on a lone rock, but at daybreak we discovered we were on the coral reef of Oeno Island, a low strip of sand about half a mile in circumference, covered with scanty growth of shrubbery. Our first fear was that the island was inhabited by cannibals, as were many of the neighboring islands, but on close inspection we found our source of alarm was groundless. We immediately set about securing our provisions, fearing the ship might break up. Occupied all day boating provisions ashore, though at great risk of swamping our boat in the heavy surf. By sunset all were landed. I left the ship in the last boat. When we finally landed, found two tents had been built (out of the wrecked ship's sails). My feelings as I looked off to the ship were of the saddest character. There lay my fine ship of yesterday, now a useless wreck. Cast upon a desolate island, my only chance of rescue being a passing vessel. I will not attempt to describe to you my feelings as I thought of home and friends. I passed the night in sleepless anxiety . . . the roar of the surf seemed to remind me constantly of our utter desolation."

On the following day Capt. Knowles walked around the island and found it a dreary waste of sand. He did find plenty of water, sea birds' eggs and fish. He also had the men rescue from the ship their livestock consisting of sheep, pigs and chickens. He also took observations and found that Oeno Island was incorrectly located on his charts by some 20 miles. Bowditch's *Practical Navigator* had not come into existence yet, and charts were often incomplete or wrong. "What a host of troubles that blunder of somebody's had made for me!" Knowles wrote in his diary.

"After consultation with Mr. B., my first officer, as to the chance of our being taken off I finally concluded to make my way to Pitcairn's Island, (where the Bounty mutineers had settled in 1789) knowing that whalers often touched there for supplies. We immediately set about rigging a boat in which to start off as soon as the surf would enable us to cross the reef."

For nearly a week the shipwreck party was held up, beset with fierce gales, rain and thunder storms. For food they made "a very palatable stew" of sea birds. They caught fish and several "pearl oysters, one of which will make a meal for a number of persons."

"Saturday, March 13th – A pleasant day but hot. In the morning I selected a boat's crew, consisting of my Mate and 6 men. At noon we set out for Pitcairn's Island, previously leaving instructions with my second officer to join me there in 4 weeks if I did not return."

As they left Oeno, Knowles stopped at the shipwreck to retrieve (without letting anyone know what he was up to) some $18,000 in gold he had hidden away there.

"A good breeze soon took us out of sight of Oeno. We now began to realize the utter helplessness of our situation. Out on the broad ocean, no land to be seen and in an open boat."

Night came on and with it a raging gale, rain and thunder. The boat nearly swamped. Using a lantern they endeavored to steer by compass, but the motion of the boat was so great this was almost impossible. By daybreak Pitcairn Island was finally sighted, Knowles estimated about 30 miles away. But the wind blew so that at times is seemed as though they made no headway at all. "Having myself done little manual labor for many years, my hands were in such condition that blood ran from my fingers' ends."

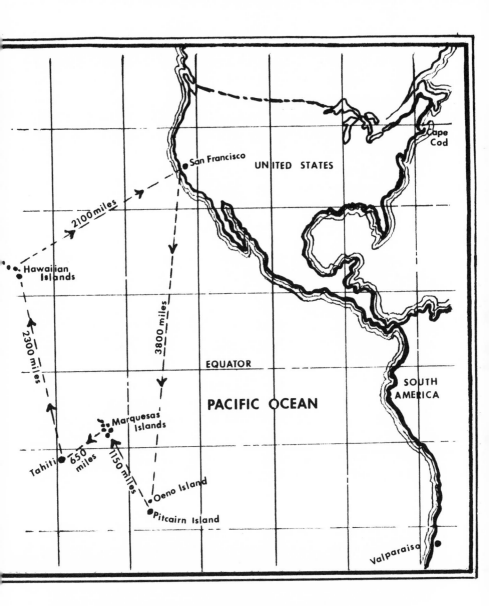

CAPT. KNOWLES WAS SHIPWRECK BOUND when he headed *Wild Wave* out of San Francisco harbor, Tue. Feb. 9. 1858, with 10 passengers and 30 crewmen aboard. This map gives some idea of the vast ocean spaces he faced. But the actual wind-dictated tacking courses he traveled could triple distances. It would be 7 months and 20 days before Knowles saw San Francisco again.

65

"Monday, March 15th – Rowed round the island but could not get in at Bounty Bay, the proper landing place. We finally effected a landing. Hauled our boat up as high as possible and started for the settlement over the mountain . . . we being obliged to crawl on all fours up the almost perpendicular heights, but finally reached the houses. To our astonishment we learned that the former residents had all left for Norfolk Island. Thus we were again on an uninhabited island. We found fruit in great abundance . . . and a good deal of livestock. Having had no rest for 56 hours we laid down to sleep, Mr. Bartlett and I each having under our heads a box of gold coins (the money rescued from *Wild Wave*)."

In the days that followed the men occupied themselves with unloading the boat, toting the stuff up the mountain, and fixing up living quarters in the abandoned houses. They found cooking utensils, picked fruit, roasted chickens on sticks over an open fire, and generally made themselves as comfortable as possible.

"Saturday, March 20th – Mr. B. took all the men out to set up a signal staff, and taking advantage of their absence, I took the gold and buried it under a flat rock on the beach."

"Sunday, March 21st – During the day we found squashes and pumpkins. We seem to be blessed with an abundance of vegetable food of the best kind. Looking for a sail today, but in vain."

The men found a good supply of axes and other tools, which would come in very handy. But their supply of matches was so low they were obliged to use flint, steel and tinder to make fires.

"Wednesday, March 24th – Mr. B. and I went to our landing place, intending to repair the boat, but to our surprise she had been stove, and not a vestige of her was in sight. We had determined to leave the island in her but this put a damper on our plans. Our prospect of getting home remained as gloomy as ever, and thoughts of the great anxiety of friends at home was a great source of sadness to me."

"Friday, 26th – It is three weeks ago since we were wrecked on Oeno Island.

"Tuesday, 30th – In the afternoon built an oven so that we might roast some meat. By digging a hole in the ground and lining it with stones and kindling a fire, we had a first-rate hot oven. Some of the men today made a sugar press."

On April 1st the men decided to build a boat and sail to Tahiti, since they had given up hope of being rescued. By April 8th the men had cut timbers and began shaping planks, which was something of a problem for they had no saws and all shaping had to be done by axe which, Knowles noted, resulted in some wastefulness of good wood. "My hands have hardened to the work day by day and I am now able to swing my axe for hours without inconvenience or pain."

"Friday, April 23rd – Seventy-five days since I sailed from San Francisco. Folks at home by this time, I fear, getting anxious not hearing of my arrival in Valparaiso.

"Saturday, April 24th – Two of us planeing and three hewing planks for our boat. Our clothing all but used up . . . it seems that we must soon take to goat skins, after the style of Robinson Crusoe. Our shoes long since gave out. We have been barefoot for a long time."

Knowles worried that the long boat, with the rest of the shipwreck crew left behind in Oeno, had not arrived, "Their non-arrival gave me great anxiety."

The island abounded in hogs and other wild stock, most so shy as to be almost impossible to catch or kill, even with good marksmanship. The men did kill a huge porker, which Knowles figured must have been the grandfather of all the other porkers. In preparation for their coming attempt to reach Tahiti, the men cut up the pig and salted the meat to preserve it They were able to gather an abundance of salt from the rocks after a heavy surf had been running, leaving pools of salt water which soon evaporated in the hot sun. They must have been reminded of the Brewster saltworks which produced tons of salt via solar evaporation.

"Wednesday, May 5th – The frame of the boat being up we set about planking her and did a long day's work. In the evening picked oakum, having on hand scraps of rope picked up here and there. (Oakum would be tapped into the seams of the boat to make it water-tight.) Large pieces (of rope) we unlaid and made into yarns with which to make rigging for the boat now building.

"Friday, May 7th – Making sails today from rags of every hue and fabric that we could find – cotton, woolen, silk or linen, from heavy canvas to thinnest sheeting.

"Wednesday, May 26th – My twenty-eighth birthday."

In order to obtain much needed nails the men set fire to one of the houses, which accidentally spread to several others. Later they picked through the rubble to gather the nails. They also made charcoal which would be needed to cook meals on their coming voyage. By June 4th the boat was finished but they still had spars to make and caulking to do. "The boat is thirty feet long, eight feet wide and four deep, having a cabin. She carries three sails and is schooner rigged. We put a pump into the boat to keep her clear of water in case she leaks. Had we plenty of good provisions we should go to San Francisco but as we have not, we intend to go to some of the islands that are inhabited nearer us."

The men found several barrels which they repaired to use for storing water on board. As July rolled around, strong winds and bad weather made it impossible to leave Pitcairn . . . and three of the men refused to go altogether, feeling chances of rescue would be better if they stayed put. To pass the anxious waiting time, the men made an ensign using red fabric from the Pitcairn church pulpit, white cotton from a shirt and blue from some dungarees. They named their boat *John Adams* after one of the original Pitcairn Island settlers.

"Friday, July 23rd – At 12 o'clock we launched the boat without disaster or mishap and anchored her off shore. Our anchor was an old anvil. Mr. B. and I went ashore and dug up our money, which had been all this time directly under the boat while building. Soon after noon weighed anchor and headed out to sea. My intention was to steer for Tahiti, but the wind being against us we headed for the Marquessas. Mr. B., myself and the crew were seasick, and had our boat swamped during the night it would have been a great effort for us to save ourselves."

The weather continued rough, the "boat very uneasy, having a peculiar motion." Twenty-four hours after setting out, Knowles recorded that they had gone 81 miles. From then on, with fair weather and good winds they were averaging over a hundred miles a day, which must have been most encouraging, since they had to travel 1150 miles across open water to reach the island of their choice!

"Tuesday, August 3rd – Sailed around the island (Ohitahoo) and stood into Resolution Bay. Having seen houses there, we thought there might be a European settlement. The natives came off in their canoes and finally surrounded us. Found there were no Europeans on the island. They (the natives) were anxious for us to anchor, but I was quite as anxious to get away, as they were a savage looking set.

"Wednesday, August 4th – In the morning saw the island of Nukahive. Not having any chart we had to sail all around the island to find the harbor, and had about given up the idea of finding a settlement. We rounded the point of the harbor, and to our great joy and surprise there lay at anchor an American Man-of-War, the only vessel in the harbor . . . it was the first ship we had seen since leaving San Francisco six months before, and this one flying the stars and stripes. We stood for the ship and hoisted our ensign. Within an hour we anchored within a few rods of her and were hailed. The Captain sent his boat off with his compliments and requested us to come on board. The ship proved to be the U.S. Sloop-of-War *Vandalia* which had only reached here the day before, and was about to leave. No American ship had been here for five years!"

"Thursday, August 5th – On board the *Vandalia*. During the morning I sold my boat (the one constructed on Pitcairn) to a missionary, receiving for her two hundred and fifty dollars."

The *Vandalia* sailed for Tahiti arriving August 10th. Here Capt. Knowles called on the American consul who offered the Captain passage aboard another sloop-of-war which was sailing for Honolulu. In Honolulu he picked up an American bark called *Yankee*, scheduled to sail for San Francisco. After long delays, *Yankee* finally put to sea and on Wednesday, September 20th "Arrived in San Francisco. On coming to anchor numerous shore boats came off, among them an old boatman who took me off to the *Wild Wave* on the 9th of February preceding. He looked at me in perfect amazement and exclaimed, 'My God! Is that you Captain Knowles?' He took me ashore. I met many old friends who welcomed me in a most hearty manner, they having long since given me up as among the missing."

On October 6th, Knowles left San Francisco for New York, arriving there on the 28th. "Here I heard from home direct for the first time, and at once telegraphed my wife in Brewster and friends in Boston."

Saturday, October 31 – "On Saturday morning started from Boston for home, where I arrived at noon. I was met at Yarmouth by Mr. Cobb with his turnout and carried to Brewster in triumph. The meeting with my family was quite affecting; such a meeting seldom takes place. Everyone had long since given me up for lost. I was indeed glad to be home and at rest."

Some years after his adventure, while on a long sea voyage, Capt. Knowles built a very special doll house for his daughter. The doll house, beautifully furnished even to including family portraits on its walls, is on display at the Brewster Historical Society Museum. The house after which it was fashioned, the former home of Capt. Josiah Nickerson Knowles, still stands today, located on Route 6A not far west of the Brewster Baptist Church.

IT WAS INDEED A PECULIAR COINCIDENCE for the two brothers-in law, Capt. Josiah Nickerson Knowles, and Capt. J. Henry Sears. At the very time Knowles' ship *Wild Wave* was wrecked on a Pacific island, and he was laboring mightily to save himself and crew, Sears' ship *Titan* was sinking in the Atlantic, with Captain and crew fighting for their lives in open longboats. And for all the bad luck of these two disasters, all hands had the good luck to survive.

23 BOXES BURIAL CASES, 881 BARRELS WHISKEY

Cargo manifests often read rather like mail order catalogs. *Glory of the Seas*, one of the new cargo-designed medium clippers, set out from New York, October 13, 1873, destination San Francisco, with her holds crammed with an astonishing mulligatawny of stuff. There were some 60,000 trunks, barrels, boxes, casks, cases, crates and kegs including 4 casks cherry juice, 2 cases gunstocks. There were 755 boxes of sewing machines and 16 bales of cambric. The hold was jammed with barrels of glue, iron pipe, lumber, matches and mirrors – nails, putty, cartons of perfumery – 300 cases each of cider and Schnapps – soap, starch, sandpaper, soda, and stoves – 6 cases of axles – tobacco, treenails, varnish, and walnuts – 18 boxes of wagons – 3 crates of crockery, 171 boxes of glassware, to name a few of the items cached aboard. It would have taken some ingenious pre-planned space allocation to stow the whiskey, cider and Schnapps out of reach, and the crockery where it wouldn't get broken.

3-MASTED TOPSAIL SCHOONER

Any vessel with two or more masts which were fore-and-aft rigged was called a schooner. They were versatile vessels. The big 3 and 4-masters were used in trans-oceanic voyages . Scaled down and modified, they were ideal for packet service, carrying passengers and cargo on coastal routes. Cape Cod fishing fleet Captains particularly favored 2-masted schooners. They were easily maneuvered by a small crew; the Captain, his Mate and four crewmen could do it, and the cook could be pressed into service if needed. Built broad of beam, the fishing schooners could carry prodigious catches of mackerel and cod.

He was a mountain of a man, a burly 6'5", a blacksmith as a lad, one of nine brothers, five of whom died at sea or in foreign ports. Through a quirk of luck and the accident of circumstance, he almost changed the history of his time. He was

SHIPMASTER JEREMIAH MAYO 1786 – 1867

For a man who so loved the adventure of a sea man's life, Jeremiah was awfully late at getting started. His father was a blacksmith and did everything he could to keep his son at home, to work with him in the business. Jeremiah managed to resist his desire to ship out until he attained the ripe old age of 16, long after most Brewster boys had gone on their first voyages and were rising up the hierarchy of command.

Mayo's first trip was a summer fishing voyage to the Strait of Belle Isle, cold, deep waters which run between Labrador and Newfoundland. When the boat returned home, Jeremiah was paid $225, his first taste of real money and its possibilities. Jeremiah Mayo gave up shoeing horses for good when he shipped before the mast on the ship *Sally*, at which job he earned $22 a month, more than any of the other crewmen. Maybe since Jeremiah was so big the Captain felt there was more of him to earn it.

The good pay was definitely an inducement for him to become a full-time sailor, but when Jeremiah got a rousing taste of the adventure of the business, money wasn't everything . . he was hooked for good. In 1805 he shipped aboard a vessel named *Industry* which was armed as protection against pirates and privateers. Along with her guns she carried salt fish to Malaga, thence to Leghorn, Alicant and Marseilles . . . then picked up a cargo of wheat and headed with it for Dublin. Near Gibraltar, *Industry* was attacked by three small lateen-rigged pirate boats probably working out of North African ports. *Industry's* Captain lost a leg in the ensuing battle and was put ashore in a hospital. Mayo was put in charge of *Industry* and brought her into Dublin on a reasonably uneventful trip. From then on Jeremiah's life at sea seemed to turn into one adventure after another.

Brewster Shipmaster Kimball Clark thought so highly of Mayo that he made him Mate on his brig *Salem*. Headed for San Sebastian, her holds overloaded with quintals of salt cod, the old brig became unmanageable and started to leak heavily from her upper seams, under the stress of an Atlantic gale and her excessive cargo. Capt. Clark, at his wits end as to how to save his ship, turned her over to Mayo with leave to do anything necessary to get *Salem* through. As the story goes, Mayo's first order of the day was to fire up the crew with liberal rations of cider. Not your store-bought pasteurized fruit juice of today, but a rousing 18th century beverage of undeniable authority. There were ship's biscuit too, all the crew could eat. Then Mayo ordered the men to bring up onto the deck three or four hundred quintals of the cod. This was no mean feat at 100 pounds per quintal. Roaring seas washing over the deck did the rest, sweeping the cod back into the briny deep from whence they had come. When *Salem's* load had been sufficiently lightened that the leaking seams rose above the water, she was brought safely into port, where Capt. Clark sold both ship and remaining cargo. And in disgust went home. Mayo stayed behind.

The brig's new French owners loaded her with claret, hired Mayo to take over, and gave him secret orders to deliver to a French port. Why secret? Because France and Britain were in the midst of one of their interminable wars, and the British navy had the French blockaded so almost nothing got in or out. Which made the demand for wine especially intense. Using false papers, a lot of Yankee bluff, and a vast amount of audacity, Mayo delivered the goods, at a huge profit to the owners, running the blockade in and out with great aplomb.

Then came the War of 1812. British ships patrolling our Eastern coast pretty much shut down all shipping. Jeremiah Mayo moored himself for the duration back home in Brewster. There to join Capt. Elijah Cobb and Capt. Kimball Clark in vociferously denouncing the war and demanding government relief for Cape sea men whose livelihoods were devastated by the blockade. Finally, no credit to Beacon Hill politicians, the war did come to an end and Mayo was back in business at sea.

Of all the challenges Mayo would face perhaps the most intriguing occurred in June, 1815, when he moored his ship in LeHavre. It is a month after Napoleon's defeat at Waterloo. The British intend to seize and exile the French Emperor. Mayo is approached by two of Napoleon's agents who ask Mayo if he will make a run for it and take the Emperor with him to the United States. The whole idea is most appealing to Mayo. It is just the kind of derring-do he loves, and he is always happy to outwit the British. Besides, he truly admires Napoleon. Mayo accepts and prepares to sail at a moment's notice. But his chance to change history is not to be. Instead, Napoleon gives himself up, and is exiled to Elba. Maybe his proverbial stomach ulcers, or his battlefield losses, had sapped his fighting spirit. Or then again, perhaps upon weighing exile to the United States vs. Elba, he preferred the shorter water route.

But just suppose Jeremiah Mayo had sneaked Napoleon aboard ship, and wined and dined him on ship's stores of cider, salt cod, and biscuit, and brought him safely to this country. Would the Little Emperor have established new headquarters for his dreams of empire on the banks of the Potomac?

Augusta Mayo, daughter of Shipmaster Jeremiah Mayo, wrote that it was the custom when a man went to sea to have his name read from the pulpit the Sunday prior to his departure, that prayers might be offered for a prosperous voyage, and upon his return home, to offer thanks for a safe homecoming.

CLEAT
A device made of metal or wood, having two arms around which a rope or line is belayed, thus holding it secure.

Our knowledge of some of Brewster's Shipmasters is to be found only in brief, cryptic and parenthetical listings in old books and town records which provide just enough information to leave us wondering. But a few of these sea men can be rescued from anonymity to be assigned their places of honor in the history of Brewster Shipmasters. Such men as:

SHIPMASTER BANGS PEPPER 1806 – 1885

Listed among the First Parish Church Shipmasters as one who engaged in the West Indian trade, he was Commander of the brig *Senator* and other ships, names now unknown. Pepper fared better than many of his fellow Masters for he lived to a hardy old age of 79 and died at home, an unusual longevity for men who earned their livings at the mercy of the sea. His home was a big, four-square house built in 1793, now painted a fine barn red, that still stands on Route 6A in Brewster.

SHIPMASTER JOHN FITZ 1856 – 1882

Served several voyages as Mate aboard the vessel curiously named *St. John Smith*. He would become her Master, and was in charge on a trip from Liverpool to San Francisco with a cargo of coal when the ship disappeared . . . probably burned at sea when her cargo of coal caught fire through spontaneous combustion, an all too common fate in those times.

SHIPMASTER ELKANAH WINSLOW 1802 – 1851

Was only 49 years old when he died in Manzanilla, Mexico, causes unknown. Thus his name is added to the calamitously long list of Brewster men, lost at sea or in foreign ports, who would never again greet families and friends. Winslow commanded the schooners *Carbine*, *Vinton*, and *Watchman*, and the bark *Sabra* . . . names which all by themselves greatly stimulate the imagination.

TOPSAIL SCHOONER

This is a two-masted vessel. The mainmast has a fore-and-aft mainsail, and a gaff topsail identical to those of an ordinary schooner. Both masts are made with two spars. The lower foremast is a little shorter than the corresponding spar of the mainmast, and the topmast as little longer. The foremast and its sails are the same as the mainmast of a brigantine, i.e. a fore-and-aft topsail, above which are yards carrying square fore-topsail and fore-topgallantsail. If you wonder why ships were designed in such a variety of shapes, rigs, and sizes, think of it in terms of today's automobiles . . . transportation designed to fit all kinds of performance and cost requirements. And to dazzle the potential buyers a bit.

The year was 1864. The place, India. The ship, *Joseph Holmes*. Her Master Charles Crosby is dead of a gunshot wound. That's where

SHIPMASTER GODFREY HOPKINS 1832 – 1902

comes on the scene. He takes over the dead Captain's ship in Bassein, India, and brings her safely home. And there our knowledge of the story ends, leaving only the intriguing mystery of the circumstances surrounding the fatal gunshot.✽

Captain Hopkins had also commanded the ship *Australia*, lost at sea near the port of Akayab. And he later would be in charge of the *William Brown* (undoubtedly so uninspiredly named after her builder, who was also into steamship building, in keeping with the growing trend to steam power). *William Brown* was on her way to Galveston, Texas, when she was lost in a hurricane in the Gulf of Mexico, only six years after Capt. Hopkins' original take-over of the deceased Capt. Crosby's command. Had *William Brown* been under steam instead of canvas could she have ridden out the hurricane? When star-crossed Shipmaster Hopkins had finally had enough of the shootings and sinkings at sea, he retired to Brewster, thereafter lending his hard-won knowledge of the world to the more mundane matters of town government, which in themselves can navigate some dangerous reefs and intricate courses!

---

15 SHIPMASTERS named Crosby . . . 13 named Foster . . . 7 named Lincoln are listed in J. Henry Sears' book of Brewster Shipmasters. And that is only a brief sampling of who was who in town. Sears does not mention one family where 9 sons were all at sea, 5 dying there. Some early Brewster families had more seawater than blood in their veins.

* CROSBY HIMSELF IS NOT AT ALL A MYSTERY.
He lives on in a popular old photographic portrait, often
described as a picture of three Brewster Sea Captain brothers. A cockey Captain Charles Crosby poses at the left,
sporting a stovepipe hat, high fashion in President Lincoln's
day. To the right is his brother Captain James Crosby, wear-
ing a matching topper. Both are definitely upstaged by the
unknown gentleman in the middle, of apparant good circumstances, for he displays a natty satin waistcoat!

He was born in Yarmouth in 1837, but

SHIPMASTER ALBERT DUNBAR 1837 – 1892

was destined to become a true Brewster Shipmaster. For his family moved to Brewster when he was just a lad. And here he would be infused with the special salty spirit of the sea men of this Cape Cod town. Dunbar left remarkably little information about himself. But it is safe to assume that he started on his life voyage, as did the other Master-bound Brewster lads, as a trainee cabin boy. By the time he was 22 or 23 Dunbar would have been closely observed by J. Henry Sears' shipping partners.

When they put the swift clipper ship *Grecian* on the line, Dunbar is given command, and she is his for all her brief life. *Grecian* is built for speed. Dunbar is a driver. It's a match made in Master's and underwriters' heaven.

Showing off her speed and the skills of Shipmaster Dunbar, *Grecian* will travel from San Francisco to Queensland, Australia in a then remarkable 102 days. If this does not sufficiently prove *Grecian's* qualities, Dunbar will take her from Cardiff, Wales, to Hong Kong in 104 days. But *Grecian's* glory will be short. She will wing her way on a total of only 6 more round trips from American ports . . . three to San Francisco, two to Hong Kong, and one to Yokohama. Then comes the fateful March day when Dunbar is bound from the Philippines to New York. *Grecian* strands on the Great Danger Reef off the island of Balaban. She is a total loss, her salvage value only $600. However, all hands are saved, brought to shore then shipped off to Manila for passage home.

When Captain Dunbar finally retired he lived out the rest of his allotted 55 years in San Diego. Captain Dunbar, no matter where you were born, or died, you are still unequivocally a genuine Brewster Shipmaster.

SHIPMASTER GEORGE CROCKER 1820 – 1883

Captain Crocker commanded the clipper *Expounder* in 1871. She was the same ship that both Josiah Nickerson Knowles and Capt. Nathan Foster had taken on flying trips around the Horn. When Crocker took her over, she was a well-seasoned vessel with 15 profitable years of business, under the banner of J. Henry Sears and Company shipping line. She would go on for an extraordinary total of 50 years, outliving all her Brewster Shipmasters.

Such an age was extremely rare for sailing vessels. Frequently their driving Masters would strain and overwork them, and their glory days would be gone in a few years. Then bad luck or bad weather on a voyage would take them to the bottom of the sea, leaving no trace of Captain, crew or cargo. Or the old hulks, no longer profitable to operate under sail, would be dismasted and turned into barges. Or hauled ashore, there to be stripped of anything of value, and left to rot.

Capt. Crocker was in charge of the ship *Electra*, on passage from Batavia to Manilla, when his luck ran out and he too died at sea. Cause unknown.

A SPLICE
Where one piece of rope is attached to another by interweaving the strands. Splicing is most durable and eliminates the use of bulky, awkward knots.

BREWSTER SHIPMASTERS WERE NEVER AT A LOSS for self-confidence. One Captain, captured by pirates, so beguiled them that they put him in charge of navigating their ship while they went below for a bit of carousing. He promptly steered the vessel onto nearby flats, where it was seized by jubilant locals.

C APE COD BAY
was the highway linking Brewster
to the rest of the world and

B REWSTER'S PACKET CAPTAINS
made their era the most colorful
and enterprising in all the
Town's history . . . .

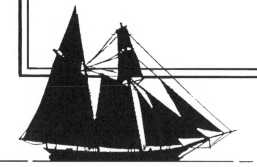

THE LITTLE CRAFT SHIVERED

and reeled under her heavy canvas, plunging and tossing as she plowed her way through gale-whipped seas. The Mate waited anxiously for the call, "Haul you gaff-topsail . . . bear a hand reefing the mainsail," but no such orders came . . . until at last, with a great crash, over went the mainmast carrying with it all its rigging. "There," shouted the Mate, "Now I hope you're satisfied, Captain Sears!"

Rounding Cape Horn? Racing for Hong Kong to win a wager over who commanded the fastest vessel? Not at all. This was Brewster's packet ship *Patriot* driving home from Boston, caught in a sudden squall-turned-gale.

We tend to overlook the vigor, character and audacious spirit of Brewster's Packet Captains. Their running lights are obscured by the dazzling performances of our roster of famed deep sea Shipmasters who sailed some of the world's fastest, finest and most fabled vessels to ports world 'round. And yet, whether Captain Tully Crosby was racing to Hong Kong on the clipper *Kingfisher*, or Captain Sears freighted goods and passengers via packet to and from Boston, both of these sea men had to reckon with the unpredictability of passage, the treachery of winds and weather and shoaling seas, and all manner of unanticipated circumstances taxing their navigational skills, ingenuity, and command to the very limit. Kittredge says of them, "The art of sailing the larger vessels was very different from the trick of handling the little two-masters. Both were high arts, but of a different sort."

The first we learn of the Brewster Packet Line is of the sloop *Five Sisters* in charge of Captain Heman Griffin, which was wrecked on rocks off Sandwich early in the 1820s. She was replaced by the sloop *Fame,* which was probably on line in 1823. An old record states: "At a meeting of the proprietors of the packet *Fame,* holden on Wednesday evening the 25th of Feb. 1824, it was voted to have the cabin of the packet cleansed, painted and varnished where she now lies as soon as the weather will permit of its doing."

Brewster's packet service was discontinued in winter and the vessels brought up the creeks, probably Quivet and Paine's Creek. Elijah Cobb, one of the packet company proprietors, wrote in a letter that in March "the packets would be able to leave as soon as tides swell sufficiently to float them down creek."

At a meeting three days later it was "voted that Captain Solomon Foster be asked if he will go in the packet the coming season on these terms: "5 per cent on the gross of stock and one half of the remainder . . . the 5 per cent allowance is in consideration of his accounting for every article of freight of every description whatever . . ."

While these records concern activities of the first organized commercial packet service in Brewster, providing reasonably regular transportation to and from Boston, from early on the people of this area had been sailing their small boats to do business in Plymouth and Boston. As rugged as it could be, the water passage of 23 leagues from this village to Boston would have been far easier, faster, and decidedly preferable to the 84-mile journey by land . . . days of exhausting, bone-jarring travel through deep-rutted sand tracks.

Despite the total lack of a harbor of any description in Brewster, the Captains of packets and coasting vessels somehow managed to cope with the difficulties of shallow water, miles of sand flats at low tide, and an anchorage exposed to the full sweep of waves across Cape Cod Bay.

Pressures to do something about a "harbor" must have increased steadily over the years, particularly as the reliability of shipping, or lack of it, touched a tender spot in the pocketbooks of local business entrepreneurs. Brewster's unique industrial area, indicated on maps as "Factory Village", the only place of its kind on the Cape, would have increasingly needed more and better shipping facilities to carry products of its boot and shoe manufacturer, tanneries, wool carding, and blanket mill and other busy enterprises. An 1837 list of the Town's economic wealth indicates the cotton mill, powered by Stony Brook, wove 192,400 yards of material. The shoe factory produced 625 pairs of boots, 3,658 pairs of shoes, and employed 17 people. Three tanneries processed 2,160 hides. And an ax maker produced 1,400 axes. There was a chair and cabinet maker, a tinware maker, 8 lamp black makers. Lamp black was in demand for the black paint used on the hulls of ships. Among unpaid laborers were 944 head of sheep which yielded 2,360 pounds of wool worth $991.00, big money in those days.

Intriguing traces of an old cartway, leading from Factory Village to the shore, pass near Brewster's windmill and the Harris-Black House located next door. Largely obliterated now by time and development, this cart path must have provided something of a highway for, among other things, wagonloads of tanbark shipped from down Maine, destined for Factory Village tanneries. Probably Glauber salts, produced at the salt works lining Lower Road shores, also needed in the tanning process, were hauled up the road to the vats. Back down would come some of those blankets, boots, shoes, axes, chairs and cabinets, heading for the nearest packet to freight them off to Boston, or to other ports where prices might be better.

All along the shore the salt works grew steadily in productivity and economic importance from their very start around 1800. Cape Codders, ever ingenious in times of adversity, began manufacturing their own salt in response to outlandish salt taxes imposed by the British. Early on, salt was made by boiling down kettles of seawater, over wood fires. Even before 1800 firewood was in short supply on the Cape. So the salt makers fastened upon the idea of solar evaporation. Sea water was pumped into square pine or cedar wood vats that measured 16′ by 16′ with rims 9″ to 12″ high – in salt works terms 16 feet of vat. Parson Simpkins, in his 1806 "Topographical Description of Brewster", noted that there were 60,000 to 70,000 feet of salt works in this town alone!

PUMPING MILLS AND WOODEN PIPES appear to be crude but represent some very capable hydraulic engineering.

SALT WORKS VATS were pretty much abondoned by late 1850s. Photo shows still intact the great roofs which were rolled aside in sunny weather. One Cape town used a signal system when bad weather threatened. Ringing church bells brought townspeople rushing to roll roofs into place.

SALT CARTED UP TO FACTORY VILLAGE could be ground at the old grist mill (large building at right) then returned to the waiting packet ship. The grist mill burned in 1870 when the miller rigged up a couple of barrels inside the mill to smoke herring, then went home to noontime dinner. When he returned, the mill was ablaze. Today's Stony Brook Mill was constructed of old salt works timbers, upon the empty foundation shown here to the left of the S-curve on Stony Brook Road.

Little wooden windmills, clattering busily in the shore breezes, were the water pumps. Their wooden pipes extended out onto the beaches at Wing's Island, and along Lower Road shore line, there to suck up the sea water as tides permitted.

Several types of salts were manufactured by this method. Using a process of decanting the brine from one vat to another, the different types were extracted. They included edible salt, Glauber's salts (which were used in tanning hides) and "bitter water" from which Epsom salts were produced. When thoroughly dried, salt to be used for cooking or table purposes was often ground (this brought better prices) before being shipped to market. Some destined for grinding may have gone up the old cartway to the Stony Brook water mill. Some may have been taken to Brewster's c.1795 windmill, whose stones are furrowed with an unusual grooving pattern possibly used for grinding salt. There was at least one salt warehouse on Lower Road where the product would be stored until a full packet load could be made up for shipment to market.

So vital was the business to the economy of the Town of Brewster that, during the War of 1812, British Commander Richard Ragett targeted the works for a ransom scheme. Anchoring his ship *HMS Spencer* close into shore, he sent a messenger with a note warning, "I call upon you to come forward with a contribution for the preservation of your salt works, which as I consider of great public utility, will be otherwise destroyed." And, "For the valuable consideration of four thousand dollars . . . we guarantee the safety of the salt works."

Captain Elijah Cobb, recognized in town as something of a sharp financier, and fully aware of the dollar loss of such a bombardment, suggested the ransom be paid. It was. And Brewster's salt-making industry continued to prosper so greatly that, by 1837, records indicate there were 60 salt-making establishments, all in need of the Packet Captains to carry their product to market.

But Brewster's salt-making industry was soon to fade away. In the 1850s railroad lines were extended into upper New York State where there were immense reservoirs of salt . . . much more easily processed than sea salt, and much more cheaply sent to markets by train than by packet boat. Eventually the Brewster salt works were dismantled and the wood used in various local buildings. The present Stony Brook Mill building (constructed in 1872 after the original structure burned) is made of salt works timber. Walls and studding are white with salt that leached out of the wood as it dried.

Even before the North Parish of Harwich separated from the South Parish in 1803 to be incorporated as the Town of Brewster, the need for a real harbor was well recognized, the only anchorage being miles of sand flats. Thus in 1804, the new young town, but a year old, decided to tackle the problem. A committee was appointed to "examine the shore and fix a most eligible spot for (creating) a harbor". By 1812, with still no harbor solution, and the threat of war with Britain very real, the development of some sort of harbor to protect local packets and other vessels was all the more urgent. And so "liberty" was granted to a company "to cut, without expense to the Town, a canal from Quivet Creek to Mill River" (Stony Brook – Paine's Creek). This endeavor also never came to fruition.

But the lack of a harbor did not stop Brewster's canny, business-minded packet proprietors from drumming up trade. In 1824, with the assignment of the packet ship *Fame* to Captain Solomon Foster's command, the proprietors authorized him to procure a "Ball and Jack with stars". The "Ball" (which may have been a large, painted barrel) would be run up a tall flagstaff located on the highest hill in Brewster, probably today's Tower Hill area, thus signalling the sighting of an incoming packet from Boston. The "Jack with stars", which was a flag, was flown at low tide, signalling that the packet would be sailing at the next high tide. When a vessel docked at night, a burning barrel of tar or pitch could be hoisted up, or a great bonfire lit, a signal easily seen across the then treeless Cape. From as far away as Chatham and Harwich passengers came to board Brewster's packet, some traveling down Stony Brook Road by stagecoach to the packet landing.

With no other way of letting the population know of ship sailings, signal poles were of great importance, not only to Brewster packets, but all along the Cape. Henry Thoreau, on his famous 1849 trip down the Cape, stated that every high eminence had a pole with signals or a sail on it. He said, ". . . it must absorb the greater part of old clothes on Cape Cod, leaving few rags for peddlers." So not all signal poles boasted a "Ball" and "Jack with stars" like Brewster's.

In the 1820s, with Brewster's economy booming, there was a definite need for more, and more frequent, trips to move passengers and cargo. The Packet Line proprietors were exploring the business potentials of forming a union with owners of the packet *LaFayette* "in order for *LaFayette* and *Fame* to run in line." This must have been the historic moment for Brewster when packet sailings, that had been intermittent and casual at best, were organized into a full-fledged shipping line, with two vessels scheduled to ply regularly (that is, as regularly as tide and weather would permit) between Brewster Landing and Boston. Captain Myrick, in charge of *Lafayette*, made frequent runs to the salt works at Robbin's Hill to load up with this salty "gold" for transportation to market. Captain Nathan Foster's commission on *Fame* was primarily to carry passengers and freight to Boston.

In 1830, as business continued to grow, Captain Luther Sears was authorized to take *Fame* to Boston and there "sell such vessel for the most she will sell for." *Fame* had served the line for six years. Now the demand was for a bigger vessel with greater capacity for both passengers and freight. That vessel, to be named *Patriot*, was being built in Charlestown. Chances are that, having sold *Fame*, Captain Sears boarded *Patriot* and took her on her maiden voyage, straight home to her new port, the Brewster flats.

Captain Sears was known for being something of a driver. Among his fellow Captains he probably never lived down his role in the dismasting of *Patriot* when he doggedly drove her home through raging seas (as was his situation when you first met him at the start of this narrative about Brewster's truly colorful Packet Captains).

But as a driver, Sears would have been a profit maker for the Line. In one sailing season he set a record with 50 round trips to Boston. That's 100 trips coming and going. For a while he was making 3 trips a week!

In 1834 Captain Sears retired. His Mate Barney Paine became Captain Barnabas Paine, taking command of *Patriot*. Captain Paine had a reputation for his almost uncanny navigating skills, no matter how dark or foggy the passage. One story tells of him being homeward bound in a great equinoctial storm when it was impossible to see an object at arm's length. His vessel was laboring so heavily that the helmsman was hard pressed to maintain course. The Captain, loathe to lay to, kept the vessel running as close to the wind as possible. When asked, "Where are we now, Captain?" he replied, "Can't tell, but I'm going home." Finally, in the inky darkness of the night *Patriot* struck fast and firm. "Cape Cod sand!" shouts Captain Paine. And sure enough, when daylight dawned, he found his craft well in shore, just below the back door of his own home. (This was probably the beach below the handsome old Cape house which still stands on Paine's Creek Road, with a commanding view of the Bay.) Barney Paine was but one of the special breed of Packet Captains who seemed instinctively to know always where they were, no matter how disorienting the circumstances.

With Brewster's Packet Line flourishing, the need for a still larger vessel was answered when the Line acquired the Packet *Sarah* and placed Captain Paine in charge. Shortly thereafter , the Line added the newly built schooner *Chatham* to the fleet, Captain John Myrick in command. Noted for his pleasant personality, Myrick was a special favorite with Brewster ladies who frequently commissioned him to bring back bonnets and other pretties from the city, or to deliver their letters to Boston. Brewster had no daily mail service back then.

It was a time when rivalries ran high between Captains, with each seeking to outdo the other in speed of trip. While *Chatham* was still on the ways being built, it was understood by her builders that if she did not outrun her rival *Sarah* they would build another packet ship that surely would.

Picture the bustle and excitement at sailing time at Brewster's boatwharf. There could be 50 or 60 passengers boarding horse-drawn sea-going wagons, built high sided and water tight like boats, to carry them out to the waiting vessels anchored in deep water. The drivers would be calling "Have a kerridge . . . have a kerridge!" to entice their trade . . . the horses would be making time as best they could against water up to their bellies, pulling their passenger loads, in a veritable parting of the seas, to *Sarah* or *Chatham*. The wharf would be piled high with freight being manhandled into the Line's three freight carts, each hauled by a yoke of oxen with a horse hitched afore. Pulling their mightiest they dragged cargo to their assigned packets amidst the yells of their drivers. Adding to all this organized chaos were the wagons of those who carted their own freight out to the waiting vessels.

Imagine the noise, the color, the cheers and jeers of onlookers – the passing of good-natured banter – the bets as to who would make port first. If the wind blew fairly there would be splash and wet, and occasionally something falling into the drink followed by appropriate curses. Then finally, with all loaded and aboard, the quick commands of Captain Paine and Captain Myrick – the creaking hoisting of sails set into a freshening breeze. Then *Chatham* and *Sarah* slip mooring and slide out into the Bay (it was called Barnstable Bay then) and are watched with searching eyes as they become specks of sails tacking their race course to Boston.

By 1845 so busy was traffic of carts and wagons, freight, and passengers-to-be, plus multitudes of onlookers going to and from the packet landing, that the Town of Brewster petitioned the County Commissioners to lay out a proper road to the landing, sandy ruts being all that served at the time. That road, still mightily busy during "the season," has variously been called the County Road, Packet Landing Road, Tupelo Road (for the handsome trees lining

PARSON SIMPKINS WITNESSED PACKET LANDING TRAFFIC
as it hustled and bustled past his parsonage on Breakwater Road in
Brewster. The 4-chimneys, 8-fireplaces home was a rare luxury on
Cape Cod where most dwellings were heated by a single great fire-
place/oven in the kitchen, Whether the Parson employed all 8
fireplaces, one in each room, is unsure, for he wrote in 1806 that
Cape Codders, suffering dire firewood shortages, were learning to
cut and burn peat. Simpkins served the First Parish Church from
1791 to 1831. The parsonage was demolished in 1859 to make
room for Shipmaster William Freeman's mansion, which still stands
today proudly overlooking Brewster's last remaining horse trough
and a little park affectionately called "The Egg" – and the hustle
and bustle of Breakwater Road.

its way in an otherwise treeless landscape), and currently Break-water Road.

For all this tremendous activity, it wasn't until 1848 that Brewster finally got its harbor, with construction of a breakwater. It was located several hundred feet off shore. Built of boulders lined up like a stone wall, the breakwater did just as its name implied . . it broke the rough waters of incoming waves, thus providing protection for Brewster packets anchored in its lee. The Line's Captains must have sighed deeply with relief.

Traces of the breakwater can still be seen at low tide from Break-water Landing at the end of Breakwater Road. And, in this same vicinity, on the shore are partially buried remnants of a corduroy road built with logs cut 5′ to 6′ long, laid close side-by-side to "pave" the soft marsh mud, possibly used by wagons driven to and from the packets.

Captain Paine hardly had time to enjoy the benefits of the new harbor when, in 1849, he fell from some barrels piled on the wharf and was so disabled that Captain Freeman Bangs took over *Sarah*. If you have ever chuckled at the true tale of the early airplane pilot nicknamed "Wrong Way Corrigan" who somehow, in an attempt to break a flying record, flew his plane east instead of west, you will empathize with Captain Bangs' trials. He was bringing *Sarah* out of Boston one night in a fair, strong breeze, with prospects of a quick trip home. Suddenly the wind swung about and the Captain found himself battling a howling gale. By midnight, when off Scituate, *Sarah* labored so fearfully that Captain Bangs put back for safe anchorage in the lee of George's Island. But even there *Sarah* could not hold her anchor, and all the Captain could do was let *Sarah* drag anchor and ride it out. Some time before dawn *Sarah* struck land head on and was awash in heavy seas. Daylight showed Captain Bangs that *Sarah* was fast ashore on Long Island.

It seems ironic that Brewster's harbor-cum-breakwater, so long in coming, (44 years, in fact, from the appointment of the first Harbor Study Committee), was so quick to lose its importance in the fortunes of the Town. The busy business of packeting, then the only reasonable way to get there from here, the only way to carry on trade, the life blood of Brewster's bustling prosperity, was to be overtaken by steamship and railroad. In 1852 Captain Bangs and Captain Myrick witnessed the steamship *Naushon,* out of Provincetown, touch at Brewster to stow cargo and board passengers, who understandably appreciated this new travel luxury with its predictability of passage. Trips by sail that often took a full day, were now reduced to a few hours by steamship. And the vagaries of weather no longer played a major role in scheduling a journey. *Naushon* was only the first to challenge Brewster's packet line. The Old Colony Railroad extended its line from Sandwich to Yarmouth in 1854. So fierce became competition between steamer, packets, the railroad and connecting stagecoach services that a fare war ensued and you could make the trip from Brewster to Boston for 50 cents.

Sarah and *Chatham* were then sold, replaced by smaller, more economically operated vessels. Captain Enos Godfrey ran the *Eliza Jane Kelly.* Captain Nathaniel Chase commanded *Rough and Ready.* But they were on the line for only a few years. By then the salt works were shut down; there was no more profitable shipping there. Finally, in 1865 the railroad came to Brewster. What had been packet cargoes turned into rail freight. And the iron horse whistled out the most exciting and colorful era in Brewster's long and intense affair with ships and the sea.

Still, a few small vessels sailed Cape Cod Bay. Eldridge's *1870 Coast Pilot* stated that "small vessels may rest safe at any season . . . within Brewster's harbor." But Brewster's Packet Captains had come ashore for good. From then on, Brewster folks did their traveling, and carried out their business by land. Now only fishermen and pleasure boat skippers were left to wait for time and tide.

TRAINS WHISTLED GOODBYE TO BREWSTER'S PACKET SERVICE
With the grand opening of this Brewster railroad station in 1865, erstwhile packet ship passengers replaced their tide tables with time tables. Hissing, sooty, clanking, efficient trains all-aboarded passengers and swiftly delivered them and wagon loads of cargo. The precisely timed progress of their rail journeys was verified the length of the Cape as trains tooted each crossing, to be heard for miles around warning, "I'm on time, are you?" Then Brewster's canvaswinged packet ships furled sail and faded into memory.

THE NAMES OF 38 BREWSTER SHIPMASTERS

are preserved in perpetuity on brass plates affixed to the pews they and their families occupied in Brewster's First Parish Church. Though these names are but a small sampling of the hundreds of Brewster men who went to sea during the 1800s and earlier, their life and death statistics (reproduced on the following pages, from *"Shipmasters of the First Parish in Brewster"*) represent fairly those of all Cape Shipmasters.

From these bare facts you can somehow still sense the pride in great ships sailed . . . the terrors of typhoons, gunshots, and uncontrollable fevers . . . the lives of many so brief; Charles Crosby only 32, the majority in their 40s. Twelve of these men would die at sea or in foreign ports . . . a fateful statistic that ensured about one-third of Brewster's Shipmaster wives could expect to become sea widows. This daunting reality seemed not at all to have deterred Brewster men from going to sea. But it must have constantly haunted the women they left behind.

> UNLISTED and unmemorialized by the First Parish records, but with lives even briefer than those twelve lost Masters, were the names of the yet-to-be Shipmasters. Mere lads, all but anonymous . . . cabin boys 11, 12, 13 years old . . . so many dead of disease in far-from-home places . . . and lost on vast seas in shipwreck drownings. Adding yet another dimension to Brewster women's grieving.

SHIPMASTERS of the FIRST PARISH IN BREWSTER

Captain	Place & Cause of Death		Life Span	Age	Ships Commanded
Baker, Franklin	At Sea	Drowning	1802-1840	38	Unknown. In W. Indian Trade
Bangs, Elisha	Brewster	Natural	1805-1886	81	Ships *Rajah, Denmark, Faneuil Hall, Crimea*
Bangs, Elkanah	Brewster	Natural	1783-1863	80	Brig *Danube*
Bangs, Freeman H.	Brewster	Natural	1809-1866	57	Brig *Roxanna* - Ships *Joseph Holmes, Faneuil Hall, Celeste Clark*
Bangs, Hiram	Orleans	Natural	1824-1879	55	Ships *Reliance, Rienzi, Mary Bangs*
Berry, Ben. F.	Brewster	Natural	1802-1864	62	Barks *Valtrallo, Rienzi, Cochituate, Reliance*
Berry, Ben F., Jr.	At Sea	Unknown	1836-1881	45	Ships *Oxenbridge, Titan*
Clark, Isaac	Africa	Fever	1761-1819	58	Commanded first American Merchantman in White Sea, Ship *California*

Name	Place	Cause	Dates	Age	Ships
Clark, William	Brewster	Natural	1808-1888	80	Ship *Brewster*
Clark, William H.	At Sea	Unknown	1839-1883	44	Ships *Brewster, Electra* - Bark *Olive*
Crosby, Charles	India	Gunshot	1833-1864	31	Bark *Keder* Ships *Forest Queen, Joseph Holmes*
Crosby, Freeman	Brewster	Natural	1802-1861	59	Ship *Gem of the Ocean* and others. Retired early
Crosby, Freeman, Jr.	Off China	Typhoon	1831-1863	32	Ships *White Swallow, Liverpool Packet*
Crosby, Tully	Brewster	Natural	1809-1891	82	Brig *Old Colony* - Bark *Arab* Ships *Monterey, Charlotte* Clippers *Kingfisher, Antelope*
Crosby, Tully, Jr.	Brewster	Natural	1841-1906	55	Ship *George Darby*
Crosby, James	At Sea	Unknown	1796-1834	38	Unknown. In W. Indian & So. American Trade
Crosby, James E.	Melrose	Cold	1838-1894	56	Ships *Oscar, Magnet, Imperial*

SHIPMASTERS of the FIRST PARISH IN BREWSTER

Captain	Place & Cause of Death	Life Span	Age	Ships Commanded
Foster, Francis Bailey	At Sea	Unknown	1842-1886	44	Bark *Celeste Clark* Ships *Kentuckian, Nonantum*
Foster, Jonathan	Brewster	Natural	1790-1862	72	Ship *Konuhassett* & others unknown.
Foster, Nathan F.	At Sea	Drowning	1833-1874	41	Ships *Expounder, Centaur,* *Morning Star, W.B. Dinsmore*
Freeman, Benjamin	Brewster	Natural	1808-1884	76	Ships *Ellen Brooks, Coromandel,* *Scargo, Climax*
Freeman, Charles	Brewster	Natural	1822-1890	68	Whaling Ship Master
Freeman, John	Brewster	Natural	1800-1864	64	Bark *Arab* - Ship *George Thacher*
Freeman, John, Jr.	Brewster	Natural	1835-1900	65	Ships *Kentuckian, Sybil* Barks *National Eagle,* *Guy G. Goss, Pilgrim*

Name	Burial Place	Cause	Dates	Age	Ships
Freeman, Solomon	Brewster	Natural	1800-1887	87	Brig *Margaret* - Ship *Malabar*
Hopkins, Charles	At Sea Buried Havana, Cuba	Unknown	1835-1866	31	Clippers *Kingfisher*, *Mountain Wave*, *Santa Claus* Brig *Loranna*
Hopkins, Godfrey	Brewster	Natural	1832-1902	70	Bark *Carib* - Ships *Joseph Holmes*, *Australia*, *William Brown*
Knowles, Elijah	Brewster	Natural	1829-1882	53	Bark *Lillie* - Ships *White Swallow*, *Nonantum*, *Landseer*
Knowles, Winslow	Brewster	Natural	1789-1870	81	Ships *Chile*, *Sophia*, *Cocuimbo*, *Albatross*
Lincoln, Joseph	At Sea	Peritonitis	1825-1870	45	Barks *Mist*, *Maria*, *Aurelia* Father of the author Joseph C. Lincoln
Lincoln, Warren	Brewster	Natural	1810-1900	90	Brig *Draco* - Bark *Mary*
Mayo, Jeremiah	Brewster	Natural	1786-1867	81	Brigs *Salem*, *Sally* - Schooner *Laury*

SHIPMASTERS of the FIRST PARISH IN BREWSTER

Captain	Place & Cause of Death		Life Span	Age	Ships Commanded
Nickerson, Fred	Boston	Natural	1808-1879	71	Vessels in Surinam and So. American Trade.
Nickerson, Joseph	Brewster	Natural	1804-1880	76	Ship *Kentucky* and others unknown. Ship *Chandler* in later life.
Pepper, Bangs	Brewster	Natural	1806-1885	79	Brig *Senator* and other ships not known. Engaged in W. Indian Trade.
Sears, J. Henry	Brewster	Heart	1829-1912	83	Ship *Faneuil Hall* Clippers *Titan*, *Wild Ranger*
Sears, Joseph H.	Brewster	Natural	1801-1885	84	Packets *Combine*, *David Porter* Schooners *Atlas*, *Cornelia* Ships *Asia*, *Faneuil Hall*
Winslow, Elkanah	Manzanilla Mexico	Unknown	1802-1851	49	Schooners *Carbine*, *Vinton*, *Watchman* - Bark *Babra*

NOW TO FAST FORWARD A BIT. The year is 1938, and Brewster is to experience the kind of excitement the Town hasn't seen since the Packet service came to an end. A ship master of another sort, named Arthur Coakley, who pilots a Luscomb airplane, (and on other days is the E. Brewster Postmaster) institutes Brewster's first and only air mail service. His landing field, the old, original Brewster golf course, now part of Ocean Edge.

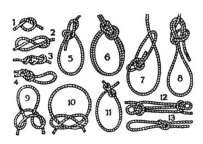

PRINCIPAL KNOTS
USED BY SEAMEN

1. Overhand 2. Figure-of-eight
3. Stevedor's 4. Loop 5. Bowline
6. Bowline on a bight 7. Running bowline 8. Bowline with a bight
9. Harness 10. Prolonge 11. Slide
12. Sheepshank 13. Slipknot

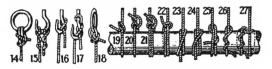

14. Anchor 15. Cat's-paw 16. Single 17. Double Blackwall
18. Studding-sail tack 19. & 20. Half hitches 21. Rolling
22. Round turn and half hitch 23. Clove hitch 24. Magnus hitch
25. Studding sail halyard 26. Timber hitch 27. Timber and a half hitch

28. Reef knot 29. Granny
30. Single 31. Double bow knot 32. & 33. Surgeon's knot 34. Becket, sheet or hawser bend 35. Double sheet 36. Englishman's tie
37. Single 38. Double, Carrick bend

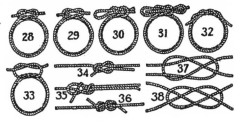

This collection touches but briefly
on a few of the colorful Shipmasters
of Brewster, who lived lives of hardship,
danger, loss and triumph we can hardly
fathom these days. Using the following
list of sources you can savour in detail
what life at sea was really like in the
age of wooden ships and iron men.

Joan Paine
Author & Designer
C.E. 2000

LINES OF CREDIT

BREWSTER PACKET LINES
From the Pilgrim Club Records – 1894
Written by Hannah Snow Collins

BREWSTER SHIPMASTERS
J. Henry Sears – 1909

SHIPMASTERS of the FIRST PARISH BREWSTER
Roger E. B. Randall – 1975

SHIPMASTERS of CAPE COD
Henry C. Kittredge – 1935

TOPOGRAPHICAL DESCRIPTION OF BREWSTER
Rev. John Simpkins – 1806

LOOKING AFT
A personal history of the family of
Capt. J. Henry Sears, by Henry Sears (Pete) Hoyt – 1997

LETTERS of CAPT. ELIJAH COBB – 1819

DIARY of CAPT. WILLIAM FREEMAN – 1874

DIARY OF CAPT. JOSIAH NICKERSON KNOWLES

THE late WALTER BABBIT
For his contagious passion for Brewster history &
the many records, notations, maps & odd tidbits
of information sent the author's way.

PAUL HUSH
For his enthusiasm and encouragement, and for taking
in tow the laborious details of editing and production.

PHOTOGRAPHS
Brewster Historical Society

Photographs courtesy Brewster Historical Society

Katahdin Ship Portrait – private ownership

Line drawings: Anchor – Capstan – Chock – Cleat –
Common Octopus – Deadeye – Seamens' Knots –
Sextant – Shrouds & Ratlines – Splice –
Right Whale.
Full-rigged Ship – Hermaphrodite Brig
Adapted from Webster's Collegiate Dictionary
Fifth Edition, G. & C. Merriam Co., Publishers
Springfield, Mass. 1936

Quotations from Rev. John Simpkins' *Topographical Description of Brewster, 1806*
Published by the Massachusetts Historical Society
Boston, Mass. VOL. X 1809

Ship silhouettes from: *Shipmasters of the First Parish in Brewster*
By Roger E. B. Randall, Oct. 19, 1975

Quotations form the diary of Shipmaster Josiah Nickerson Knowles,
pertaining to the wreck of the Wild Wave – private ownership

Shipmasters of Cape Cod by Henry C. Kittredge
Houghton Mifflin Company
The Riverside Press, Cambridge 1935